ON THE
DIVINE LITURGY

ORTHODOX HOMILIES

VOLUME TWO

THE MOST REVEREND METROPOLITAN
AUGOUSTINOS N. KANTIOTES

AUGOUSTINOS N. KANTIOTES
Bishop of Florina, Greece

ON THE
DIVINE LITURGY

ORTHODOX HOMILIES

VOLUME TWO

Translated and Foreworded
by
ASTERIOS GEROSTERGIOS

INSTITUTE FOR BYZANTINE AND MODERN GREEK STUDIES
115 Gilbert Road
Belmont, Massachusetts 02178

On the Divine Liturgy, Orthodox Homilies, originally appeared in Greek under the title, Εἰς τὴν Θείαν Λειτουργίαν, Πρακτικαὶ Ὁμιλίαι , published by the Orthodox Missionary Brotherhood, "Ὁ Σταυρός" ("The Cross"), Athens, 1978. The author dedicated this second volume "To those who receive regularly,'with fear of God, with faith and with love,' the Body and Blood of Christ." We dedicate this translation, as we did that of Volume One, to the author on the occasion of his fiftieth anniversary as a clergyman-preacher of the Orthodox Church, with deep reverence and love, expressing our gratitude for his kind permission and encouragement toward the translation and publication of this work.

Copyright © 1986, by Asterios Gerostergios
Published by THE INSTITUTE FOR BYZANTINE
AND MODERN GREEK STUDIES, INC.
115 Gilbert Road, Belmont, Massachusetts 02178, U.S.A.
Library of Congress Catalog card Number: 86-080941
Printed in the United States of America

Complete set ISBN 0-914744-71-2
This volume ISBN 0-914744-73-9

TRANSLATOR'S FOREWORD

The present volume, *On The Divine Liturgy* by Augoustinos N. Kantiotes, Bishop of Florina, is a continuation of the first which dealt with the Liturgy of the Catechumens. In this volume, the author gives a point-by-point discussion of the principal part of the Divine Liturgy, the Liturgy of the Faithful.

The first volume appeared in print at the beginning of the present year. Its content has pleased many readers, some of whom sent beautiful letters with favorable comments and expressions of gratitude for the spiritual joy the volume bestowed. We hope to print some of these letters in a future edition, for they are proof of our people's hunger for Orthodox spiritual food, and we feel justified in our decision to translate and publish this particular work of the renowned author and churchman.

Bishop Augoustinos N. Kantiotes was born in 1907 in the village of Lefkai, on Paros, one of the Cyclades Islands. The child of very religious and pious parents, he was blessed throughout his youth with exceptional teachers, famous for their piety and their love for Greek classical education: Nikolaos Gaitanos, Ioannes Rosses, and Konstantinos Gavras. He graduated *cum laude* from the Theological School of the University of Athens in 1929. There, his theological education and Christian development were overseen by the famous professors Panagiotes Trempelas and Christos Androutsos, and especially two zealous Fathers with whom he had association from his early years, Archimandrite Philotheos Zervakos, abbot of the Monastery of Longovarda on Paros and Archimandrite Eusebios Matthopoulos, founder of the religious brotherhood of theologians, "Zoe."

As a layman, Kantiotes taught Grammar School for five years and was then ordained a priest in the diocese of the late Metropolitan of Akarnania, Hierotheos. He served seven years as chancellor for that diocese, preaching and organizing the diocese in an exemplary manner. In the next few years, he served as preacher in a number of dioceses in Greece, and during the Greek civil war, he served in the army. He founded more than 20 religious societies throughout the country and published an array of periodicals like *Spitha, Ho Stavros* and *Salpinx Orthodoxias.* He established boarding houses for high school and university students, and founded the religious brotherhood *Ho Stavros.* He built and renovated dozens of churches and benevolent institutions like nursing homes, orphanages, and vocational schools. He established summer camps for boys and girls where, each year, thousands of young people find spiritual direction and a healthy environment far from the polluted atmosphere of the cities. He is founder and director of an ecclesiastical school which trains future clergy. He brought new life and hope not only to his local church, where he has served as bishop since 1967, but to the whole Church. He is the guardian angel and provider of both spiritual and material aid to thousands of people. His fifteen years of service in the Greek capital (1951-1967) influenced the religious and public life of the city. And as Bishop of Florina, his extraordinary pastoral work elevated him in the minds of the faithful, who consider him a unique, great contemporary Shepherd and Teacher of the Orthodox Church.

Bishop Augoustinos cultivated the written and spoken word of God as did few other contemporary churchmen or theologians. His ascetic life, his vast education, his deep knowledge of Patristic writings and the Holy Bible formed a pure Orthodox conscience within him. Although persecuted for his critical stance against the abuses of his day, both among the clergy and the laity, he has always been justified in the end, because his criticisms reflected the will of a healthy, contemporary Church conscience.

It is to Bishop Augoustinos that we dedicate these two volumes on the occasion of his fiftieth anniversary as a clergyman and preacher of the Orthodox Church. We hope that, by God's grace, more of his writings will find their way into the English-speaking world, to help us travel the spiritual path of the life in Christ.

ASTERIOS GEROSTERGIOS

PREFACE

The Divine Liturgy is one of God's greatest gifts to man. In it, the believer not only communicates with the Triune God, but is mystically united with the God-Man, the Lord. The Divine Liturgy is a beautiful service of petitions and supplications, which involve all of man's material and spiritual needs. It is above all an offering. Man offers God the simple material gifts of bread and wine, and God offers man in return the same gifts changed into the Body and Blood of Christ. Christ, in the Divine Liturgy, is "the Offerer and the Offered and the Acceptor."

What service can compare with the Divine Liturgy? What gift can compare with the gift offered at the Liturgy, the Holy Communion? What moment in man's earthly life can compare with the moment when he receives from the mystical table of the Lord? There is no moment more holy and divine and sweet than the moment when a believer receives the Body and Blood of our Lord and Savior, Jesus Christ.

Unfortunately, this treasure we know as the Divine Liturgy is understood by only a few and appreciated by fewer still. A true believer is grieved when he sees how few people regularly attend church services. The great mass of the so-called Christians have left the home of the Father, rich in spiritual goods, and have sought to satisfy the hunger and thirst of their souls with the junk-food of secular life and sin. What a shame! Their souls waste away and die, while the Master's table is full to overflowing, and His invitation is always open: "Take ye . . . Drink all of you of this."

And as of the few people who are in church every Sunday and great holiday, do they feel the grandeur of the Divine Liturgy? Do they consciously participate in what is being said and done for them in the Liturgy? The answer for most is "no." This is obvious from the inattentive way in which they participate, as well as from the small number who regularly receive Holy Communion.

A certain mechanicalness is characteristic of the way many priests perform the Liturgy, as well as of the way the congregation responds to it. Many priests only go through the motions of performing the Divine Liturgy. They are not inspired when they stand before the Holy Altar and see the Holy Paten and the Holy Chalice of the Body and Blood of Christ. Sometimes the act of reading and musical execution of the petitions absorb all their attention so that they cannot attend to the Liturgy with the required emotional and spiritual participation ....The congregation likewise participates mechanically. The body may be present, but the spirit is elsewhere....

We must break free from this mechanicalness. We are not cold and indifferent before a table abundantly laden with good food and drink. Why then are we thus when before us, on the Holy Altar, is the sweetest and most beneficial spiritual food?

The aim of this book is to inspire sincere participation in the Divine Liturgy. This is the second of two volumes entitled *On the Divine Liturgy*. Both books reprint the collected short sermons of the Bishop of

Florina, Augoustinos, which were originally published in *Kyriake*, a pamphlet put out by the Metropolis of Florina. The first volume was concerned with the first part of the Divine Liturgy, "the Liturgy of the Catechumens." This volume deals with the second, and more important, part: "the Liturgy of the Faithful."

In a simple yet vivid way, certain points of the Divine Liturgy are interpreted for those who steadfastly believe in the mystery of the Holy Communion. The sermons are characterized by their simple style and language. They are not intended for theologians or specialists, but for the village people who are not very educated, and hence many examples are used to make the message clear. For though they are simply written, these sermons are concerned with profound theological matters.

These sermons make up a "Guide to Christ," for they are intended to lead the souls of Christians to Christ, Who is in whole on the Holy Altar, offered "as nourishment to the faithful." These sermons are meant to take the communicant and lead him up to the Beautiful Gate, where the priest holds the Holy Chalice and says: "With the fear of God, with faith and with love, draw near."

May this book so arouse Christians that they attend with reverence the Divine Liturgy, worship the true God "in spirit and truth," and participate often with faith and joy in the Holy Communion. May the beautiful hymn at the close of the Divine Liturgy be sung not mechanically, but in earnest: "We have seen the pure Light, we have found the true Faith, worshipping the undivided Trinity, Who hath saved us."

Athens, September 8, 1978
Orthodox Missionary Brotherhood of
Ho Stavros ("The Cross")

CONTENTS

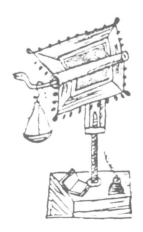

I

THE PRAYERS OF
THE FAITHFUL

"ALL YE WHO ARE FAITHFUL"

In the early days of the Church, my brothers, there was wonderful orderliness and propriety. All, like members of a disciplined army, obeyed their superiors, the spiritual fathers of the Church. And if someone did disobey, he was immediately singled out and made to suffer spiritual punishment. There was at that time a fear of God

Today, however, great disorder prevails in the churches when the Divine Liturgy is celebrated. Men and women alike enter the church shamelessly, immodestly dressed, and there is no one to bar their entrance. And if a devout priest dares to criticize these people, he is opposed by the many, who resent him and resist him and create a disturbance, asking the bishop to punish the zealot priest! If a priest wants to have good relations with everybody, so that he can be sure to collect gifts from one and all, whether believer or atheist, he must criticize no one, regardless of what commotion goes in the church. And so the priest gets along with the world. When such a priest is the celebrant, the church, as St. John Chrysostom said, is no different from any other place, such as the marketplace, where anyone can do whatever he wants.

And so, unfortunately, where there ought to be the greatest order, there prevails great disorder.

The devout priest, however, must not take the bad example of his colleagues to heart. He must work diligently, patiently, zealously, so that order may once again reign in the church. For the priest is responsible to God for whatever improprieties occur in His house.

These words on order are appropriate here, for we are about to continue our discussion of the Divine Liturgy with attention to its second and most important part, the Liturgy of the Faithful. If order must prevail during the first part, the Liturgy of the Catechumens, so that communicants can hear the petitions, prayers, readings, and sermon, it must prevail all the more when the Lord, no longer as Teacher but as Archpriest, prepares to celebrate the mystery of the Divine Eucharist, to offer His body and blood to the faithful. In this hour the church should be cleared of unbelievers. Only the faithful can participate in the mystery of the Holy Eucharist. The catechumens – i.e. those not yet baptized – and those sinners under Church penance were in early years of the Church made to leave before this part of the Liturgy. And they would leave with tears in their eyes when they heard this admonition of the deacon or the priest:

"All ye who are catechumens depart: ye catechumens depart: let not any catechumens remain."

With the catechumens gone, only a few remained. These men, women, and children were the faithful, who were to attend the second part of the Liturgy and receive Holy Communion. And the deacon addressed them saying:

"All ye who are faithful, again and again in peace let us beseech the Lord. Succour us, save us, comfort and protect us, O God, by Thy Grace."

In the early days of the Church, those who remained in the church were indeed faithful. But today, those who

remain after the admonition "All ye who are faithful. . ."
(which should be said these days not once but two and
three times) — are they really faithful and worthy to participate in the awesome sacrifice of Golgotha? Are these
the faithful, who come to church only on Christmas and
Easter? Can we call the multitudes who are accustomed come to church once or twice a year "the faithful?"
If one were to ask these people: "Why didn't you come
to church regularly?" he would expect to hear: "We don't
go to church, but we are good people."

Good people! He's good, she's good, everybody's
good! To quote an Orthodox teacher: "Hell will be filled
with. . . 'good' people!" Those people, who sign their own
certificates of merit, are sadly mistaken. For one thing,
they don't know themselves. If they were to examine
their own lives from childhood to this day, they would
find that they have often violated God's will as expressed
in Scripture. No matter how good they may appear to
be, they may be corrupt at heart and drawn towards evil.
If this evil is not expressed in acts — of prostitution,
adultery, murder, theft — then it may be for fear of being caught in the nets of human justice.

Secondly, those who claim to be good don't know
the Gospels. For the Gospels proclaim that, in order for
a man to be saved, good deeds are not enough, regardless
of how many or how great they might be. For if good
deeds alone could save a man, then it would not have
been necessary for the Son of God to come into the
world, to be crucified and to shed His precious blood.
His sacrifice would have been in vain.

Thus we are saved through faith. So said the Lord:
"Whoever believes and is baptized will be saved; whoever does not believe will be condemned" (Mark 16:16).

A thousand acts of charity cannot save the unbeliever. Faith is indispensible for salvation. The same faith is indispensible for participation in the mystery of the Holy Eucharist.

My dear brothers! We gain nothing if we go to church because it is the custom, if we go without faith in Christ. That is why the deacon proclaims before the celebration of the Holy Eucharist: "All ye who are faithful. . . ."

IN COMMEMORATION

In this world, my dear brothers, something always is happening. And of these many things, some are distinguished from the rest by their exceptional influence on the lives of men. Let us consider one event from the history of our motherland: The Revolution of 1821, which we celebrate, together with the Feast Day of the Annunciation, on March 25. The Greeks, enthusiastic, patriotic, strong in their faith, from within the deep darkness of slavery lit the light of liberty. And they kept the light burning for seven years of war. All the opposing winds and storms, the armies and navies of the Ottoman Empire, could not blow out this torch of liberty. And at last, the few overthrew the many, and Greece was set free after four hundred years of oppressive rule. The flag of the cross once again flew over the Acropolis. But the liberated territory was small. Outside the free kingdom, millions of Greeks continued to groan under the Turkish yoke. And so more battles were fought, until Greece at last stretched wide her loving wings and collected to herself most of her tormented children. Greece remains to this day a free nation of a single remarkable people.

Greece is a free nation. But how many trials, how many battles, how many sacrifices did it take to topple the tyrants, to free the people! The blood of her children flowed like a river, watering the tree of liberty whose shade we, the new Greeks, enjoy today.

They fought like lions. They overwhelmed the enemy. They liberated villages and cities. And myriads of them fell dead on the fields of bloodly battles. These heroes laid down their lives for the motherland. There isn't a city or town, however small it might be, that does not have its own glorious heroes. Men and boys in the flower of their youth, on hearing the trumpet call them to war, not for conquest but for the liberation of their enslaved brothers, left behind the joys of family life to serve in the army, to fight bravely, and to die for faith and flag.

These heroes, who sacrificed their lives for the good of all, have not been forgotten by their people. In every city and town monuments have been erected, and on them, in letters of gold stamped on marble slabs, are the precious names of these heroes. And each year on the Holy Day of the Annunciation, as the entire nation celebrates, young and old alike gather at these monuments and remember their dead with a memorial service. The heroes' names are read aloud, the national anthem is sung, and the patriots, their bodies shaken by passion, all together exclaim: "May their memory be eternal."

The human soul gratefully appreciates the sacrifices of these beneficent heroes. And, as an excellent commentator on the Divine Liturgy, Nicholas Kavasilas, observes, the human soul creates many means by which to preserve memory, such as graves, statues and other monuments, as well as holidays, games, and festivals.

We are all moved, dear brothers, whenever we hear about the heroic deeds, the self-sacrifices of great men. And yet, as we contemplate our own national heroes, let us consider: of all the sacrifices, from the dawn of history to this day, which one is the greatest and most beneficent? Your own answer to this question will show that which you most believe in. If you value your health above all things, then you will proclaim your doctor as your benefactor, for he labored to save you from the clutches of death; you might hang his picture in your room, and be moved whenever you hear his name mentioned. If your top priority is knowledge and science, and you admire inventions and discoveries, then you will proclaim some scholar or scientist who worked for the progress of technological civilization to be your benefactor. If your first loyalty is to your country, then you will top your list with those national heroes who sacrificed their lives in battle that you might be free.

Health, knowledge, science, civilization, country, freedom: are these the only good things we should acknowledge? My brothers, there is another good which is incomparably more valuable. This material world, our earth, and countless stars will be reduced to dust. One thing alone will last. And that is the soul. Yes, the soul! The soul is immaterial and immortal, and so it must outlast all that is material and mortal. There is no force strong enough to destroy the soul.

If we could see our own souls with our eyes, however, we would see that they are in sad shape. They are enslaved, held captive, locked tight in satanic chains of our terrible passions, chains which we cannot break with our knowledge, our science, our philosophy, or revolution. Man may appear to be free in body, but his soul is always bound by his sins. In all lands, in all epochs, man has sought true deliverance. The painful truth is that man alone cannot free himself to live in the garden of life, to breathe the air of spiritual freedom.

Who, then, sets man free? *Christ!* Christ, with the sacrifice of His precious blood, shed for us all on Golgotha, has delivered the world from evil.

Christ's sacrifice is unique. All other sacrifices are dwarfed by the supreme sacrifice of our Lord.

Christ is the king of heroes and of saints.

My dear brothers! If we set aside a time to love, honor, and remember the heroes of our nation, we must countless more times remember, love, and honor our Christ, who suffered the most horrible death for the salvation of our souls. It is that we may remember this greatest of sacrifices that the Divine Liturgy was formed. Certainly, this is as He willed it: "Do this in memory of me" (Luke 22:19).

SIN / IGNORANCE

Let us continue with our explanation of the Divine Liturgy. We begin this week with its most important part, the Liturgy of the Faithful. This is made up of the commemoration of the Lord's terrible suffering, the sanctification of the precious gifts, the partaking of the Holy Eucharist, the prayer of Thanksgiving, and the Dismissal.

The Liturgy of the Faithful opens with the deacon's admonition: "All ye who are the faithful." As we mentioned in a previous sermon, only the faithful should remain in the church from this point on. In the early Church this was strictly observed. If we were to be strict about this today, I'm afraid to think of how few would be left behind in the church.

On this, unfortunately, we are worse than pagans. Even the pagans, although they believed in false gods, felt so strongly about their gods that they excluded sinners and criminals from participation in their holiday services, festivals, and games. The herald would cry out: "Away with the adulterous, away with the profane, away with the blasphemous. Out with the impious." And so our ancestors acted to keep their services holy. And we, who have the true religion, we Orthodox Christians, full of sin and impiety, without, compunction or shame, enter the church and attend the awesome sacred service, cold and indifferent, as if it is our right and not our privilege.

Oh, if only some mighty worldly ruler would invite us to a banquet, how we would run to him, full of joy and thanksgiving for the honor, showering him with praise. . . .

"All ye who are faithful. . . ," proclaims the deacon. Then he makes a short supplication, ending with the word "wisdom." This means that what is to follow will be a testimony to the wisdom of God for the salvation of man. The priest, standing before the altar, says the first prayer of the faithful:

"'Almighty God, we give Thee thanks that Thou hast deemed us worthy to stand at this time before Thy Holy Altar, and to make our adoration before Thy mercies, both for our sins and the ignorances of the people. Receive, O God, our supplication. Make us worthy to bring supplications and prayers and bloodless sacrifices before Thee, on behalf of all Thy people, and enable us, whom Thou hast placed by the power of Thy Holy Spirit in this Service, to call upon Thee in every time and place without reproach, blamelessly, and with the witness of a good conscience, so that when Thou hearest us Thou mayest, of Thy great goodness, be merciful to us."

With his prayer the priest expressed his gratitude and the gratitude of the faithful for the great honor which God grants by allowing him, the priest, to stand in this holy hour before the altar.

The altar of our Church is unique among all the altars of the world. The priests of the ancient world brought animals to slaughter and to burn on their altars, and they sprinkled the people gathered there with the animal's blood. Even the Jews offered such sacrifices, called "bloody sacrifices," though theirs differed from the heathen's because the Jews worshipped the true God. All the sacrifices of the ancient world, however, could not save fallen mankind. They only expressed man's guilt and his longing for salvation. They were but hints and shadows of the great and unique sacrifice which Christ was to offer at Golgotha.

Oh, holy altar, awesome sanctuary! How do we, unworthy as we are, have the audacity to face you? The priest, the devout priest, who approaches the altar to begin the celebration of the Mystery, is seized with awe. He trembles and falls down before the Lord, asking for His mercy and compassion. In this sacred moment, he is moved to ask for Divine grace. He petitions the Lord on his own behalf and on behalf of his people.

"Oh, boundless and almighty God! Thou Who dost rule over natural and supernatural powers, God of Heaven and earth, we ask for Thy grace! We, Thy priests, ask this of Thee, in this holy hour, that Thou mayest accept our prayers for the forgiveness of our sins and for the ignorance of thy people."

Let us pause here and consider this prayer. Let us examine the distinction between the offences of the clergy and the offences of the people.

God gave to man the written and the unwritten law. The unwritten law consists of the Ten Commandments, the sermon on the Mount, and all the moral commandments of the Church, called Holy Canons, which are in accordance with Scripture. The unwritten law is conscience.

All of us who have been baptized and become Christians must obey the Law of God, both written and unwritten. I ask, however, do we obey? Unfortunatly, no.

Each one of us, in his own way, disobeys God's Commandments. We are all violators. The violations of the lay people are called "acts of ignorance," while the violations of the clergymen are called "sins." Why do we make this distinction? Because the people, who work hard for their living, who suffer hardships and injustices, who are attacked from all sides, sheep without a shepherd – these people are unilluminated in many things, and when they disobey God's will, many times it is out of ignorance. If we could only take advantage of all our contemporary media to illuminate these people! If they only knew, they would not commit so many sins. But now they live in ignorance – certainly not complete ignorance, but partial ignorance, which is made greater by the endless propaganda of error and sin with which they are constantly bombarded. Surely this cannot be said of the clergy. These men, who have been entrusted to lead the people, who day and night are involved with the Holy and Sacred Religion, are not ignorant. They know the will of God. And so their transgressions cannot be attributed to ignorance, as can many of those of the people, but must be acknowledged as sins.

My dear brethren! Clergy and laity alike will be judged for violating God's laws. Clergymen, however, will be judged more severely and will be punished more heavily. For he who knows more will be punished more (Luke 12:47).

THE WITNESS OF CONSCIENCE

We continue, beloved, our explanation of the first petition of the faithful. The priest, terrified before the holy altar, overwhelmed by his weakness and unworthiness, begs the Lord to forgive him for his sins and the people for theirs. He asks to be made worthy to offer the bloodless sacrifice. He prays that God may enable him to call upon Him "in every time and place without reproach, blamelessly, and with the witness of a good conscience."

The prayer refers to "conscience," specifically, the priest who is to offer the sacrament of the Holy Eucharist must have a clear conscience. But what is conscience?

Let us consider as examples two men whom we recall during Holy Week because of their involvement in Christ's Passion: Peter and Judas. Peter, the zealous disciple of Christ, boldly proclaimed that he would never betray his Lord, even if all others did. Christ, however, told Peter, "Before the rooster crows tonight you will say three times that you do not know me" (Matt. 26:34). And so it happened. On the night of Holy Thursday, while Christ was being tried before Caiaphas and Annas, Peter watched from the courtyard, his identity hidden. He watched the Divine Drama, hiding within himself his own drama.

In that terrible hour, he wrestled with his thoughts. His fear dominated him completely. No longer was he the Peter who, roused into action by the arrest of Christ, drew his sword in His defense. This Peter trembled with fear of being recognized as a disciple and arrested. Was this the same man who swore to follow Christ unto death? Three times he was pointed out by a servant of the priests and three times this frightened man betrayed his Master with curses and denials.

What was going on in Peter's conscience? Certainly his conscience existed, but in the hour of his betrayal, it was asleep. But with the crow of the rooster, his sleeping conscience awoke. Christ's words came back to him, and Peter was greatly disturbed when Christ, led through the courtyard by His captors, caught his eye. Peter's conscience came to life and protested: "Peter, what have you done?" Aware of the gravity in his offense, Peter went out into the night and wept bitterly.

Peter's conscience accused him. It told him that all was not right within him, that he had become a traitor. With the help of Divine grace, however, Peter repented, and God's peace returned to his heart.

But we have a different case: that of Judas, one of the Twelve. His sin was greater than Peter's. Peter denied Christ from fear, but Judas betrayed Him from avarice. He sold his Teacher for a humiliating thirty coins, the price of a slave. At first, when he betrayed Christ, and accepted in his hands the purse of the coins, Judas' conscience was sleeping. When he later learned, however, that Christ had been condemned, his conscience woke up. Like a stormy, troubled sea, it cast up great waves of despair, trying to drown him. Divine grace had forsaken him. Alone, completely alone, he fought the raging waves, and was overwhelmed by them. In despair, he ended his own life. He hung himself.

Judas' conscience woke up, but it was not like Peter's conscience. His was a conscience diseased, darkened, distorted by avarice. Egotists may kneel down and repent; the avaricious find it much harder to do so. Avarice petrifies the heart: it darkens and confuses the mind.

Conscience is the faculty of the soul which distinguishes good from evil. Orthodox Christian psychology teaches us that we are born with this power. It is a natural part of man's soul. Conscience, then, can be seen working in all peoples of all ages. Conscience came into being with man's creation in this world. Adam and Eve, the first to sin, felt the remorse of conscience and tried to hide from God's sight. Cain, the first murderer and polluter of the earth, could never calm himself; the voice of his conscience, calling "Cain, Cain, where is thy brother?" would not leave him in peace.

Conscience cries out in the darkness that covers the world. It cries out like the rooster in the night of Holy Thursday. Have you ever slept out in the country, at night when silence reigns? How strong and clear rings the rooster's crow! But when the wind blows through the branches and a storm rages, the rooster's call is drowned by noise. So with conscience. It crows continually. But when our passions are aroused like storms, roaring in our souls, the voice of conscience cannot be heard.

One day, however, it will be heared. God grant that it be heared in this life, for, if not, it will be endless and unbearable. It will be damnation for all time. As St. Chrysostom said, it is better to be stung by a scorpion than by conscience.

My dear Christians: let us all, and particularly our clergymen take heed of our conscience. Clergymen are, after all, human beings, and they sin too. If their sins are not grave and known by all, then let them recall whose soldiers they are; let them repent and cry like Peter. If, however, their sins are serious, be they public or private, then their consciences accuse them of being unclean and therefore unworthy to stand before the awesome altar. Should such priests continue to celebrate the Divine Mysteries? Of course not! In the days when men feared God, those priests who had committed mortal sins would hang up their stoles and perform the sacraments no more. Such priests were admirable examples of repentance. Today? Alas! Eight thousand priests celebrate the Divine Liturgy every Sunday. Can it be that, of these eight thousand, not one has committed so serious a sin that he cannot enter the sanctuary?

My dear brothers! Have pity and weep for the priests of our age, who stand unrepentant and uncaring before the holy altar.

"NOW"

After the first petition of the faithful, the priest audibly continues:

"For to Thee belong all glory, honor worship, to the Father and to the Son, and to the Holy Spirit, now and forever and from all ages to all ages."

In this reading, as well as in many others the word "now" is used. Because this word is repeated throughout, we shall base our homily on it.

What does "now" mean? In both the classical and New Testament Greek language it is *"nyn."* In modern Greek it is *"tora."* It has noteworthy meanings when used in conjunction with the "forever and from all ages to all ages."

Time, beloved, is divided into the past, the present, and the future. Imagine that we are standing on an extremely narrow strip, if you turn towards one side or the other you still only gaze at sea; a sea which extends far beyond your vision and disappears into the horizon. This narrow strip of land, where we find ourselves and just manage to get our footing, while to our right and to our left the waves of the two seas pound at our feet, is the "now." It is the present. The two oceans are the past and the future.

The ocean is vast. The past and future are also vast. If we could take a look into the past, not just the past of our own life which accounts for only a few years, but if we proceed through and open up history, we would see all that the ancient peoples have done here on earth, and proceed again further, beyond the creation of man, extend our gaze into the ages of ages, which have passed from the time when the Almighty cry was heard: "Let there be light" (Gen. 1:3), we get some idea of the past. What are we chronologically in comparison to the entire past? A drop in the ocean.

And what are we in comparison to the future, which is going to continue after our death? Our life here, in comparison to past and future time, is not even a drop in the ocean!

The man who stands in the "now," in the present, if he turns and sees his past, a past full of both small and great sins, an open sea continuously disturbed by memories, is overcome by melancholy, and cries: "My time is lost." His conscience feels remorse; it leaves him no peace. He is disturbed and trembles even thinking about the past. With various means he tries to forget, to deaden the remembrance of the past. O the past! How much anxiety this causes the sinner!

There is also the thought of the future. Does not this also cause uneasiness for men? What is going to happen to me? Which obstacles, which misfortunes, which sorrows am I going to face in my personal life, in my family life? Will I be healthy, or will I become infected with some incurable illness and suffer for a long time in a bed of pain? What will happen to me . . . ? These questions, raised from thinking about the future, arise in man's heart, and provoke uneasiness. And man, being between the past and the future, balanced on that narrow strip of the present, is in agony, which in the language of psychology is called anxiety.

How can man be freed from this anxiety of the past and the future? Glory be to Christ! Only He can save us from this terrible anxiety. He gives us medications for our salvation. One for anxiety with reference to the past, the other for the anxiety with reference to the future.

The first medicine is sincere repentance. A pit is opened up and all sins of man are buried there. And on this pit sits David, singing with his sweet lyre: "Blessed are they whose iniquities are forgiven, and whose sins are covered" (Greek Psalter 31:1, English version 31:1).

Also the uneasiness, agony, impatience and anxiety, provoked from thoughts of an unknown future, are calmed and disappear with the medicine called hope. A hope not based on persons and things of this world, but on the solid unshakable rock, the rock of ages, our Lord Jesus Christ. Christ is the only hope of the world. Blessed and fortunate are those who hope in Christ. Unfortunate are those who base all their hope in men.

But we must also pay attention to the "now." For the smallest particle of time, the moment, has great importance. Unfortunately, the majority of the people leave the "now" unexploited. Their mind is not occupied with the present, but is in reverie. It is left to dream, to make mythical fortresses and places for the future. The medicine for this indolent situation is activity, work, the satisfaction of every moment. Because for every moment there exists a duty, and we are called upon to perform it, regardless of how small it appears. I ask, what is a glass of cold water worth which someone offers to a thirsty man? Yet, the Lord said that even this small offering of the moment will not remain unrewarded (Matt. 10:42). And because our life is the sum of moments, we understand how much value every moment has; namely how much value the "now" has.

"Now and forever and from all ages to all ages." The Holy Trinity, the Father, the Son and the Holy Spirit, will never cease to be hymned in all ages. And now and always and into eternity they will be glorified, honored and worshipped. Also throughout our life, from childhood until death, it is necessary to hymn and to glorify God. Not only during the Divine Liturgy, but every hour and every moment it is necessary to honor and glorify God. How? By sanctifying every moment of our life by performing our Christian duties.

The farmer who tills and sows the earth, the shepherd who pastures his sheep, the worker who works in the factory, the employee who works in the office, the sailor who travels the sea, the officers and soldiers who guard the borders, the leaders who govern the people, the priests of the Most High who serve in church; and yes, even the invalids and bed-ridden, who are not able to work, − all without exception must pay attention to the "now" and sanctify every moment of our life.

Thus every moment will become a golden coin with the icon of Christ depicted on it.

"DEFILEMENT OF FLESH AND SPIRIT"

As we have said in previous homilies, dearly beloved, there was order in the early church; it functioned precisely, like a clock. The people could not do whatever they wished. Not everyone could even enter the church, for someone was watching at the door.

And again, not all of those who entered the church when the Divine Liturgy was being celebrated were allowed to remain till the end. The people who were not baptized, but were the catechumens, remained in church only until the Gospel reading and the sermon.* After that, obeying the admonition of the deacon, they left. Because then the most important part of the Liturgy would begin, and they were not considered worthy to attend this awesome mystery. Along with the catechumens, those of the baptized who had fallen into serious sin, and for a time had to stay away from Holy Communion, would leave. As well, those who were demonized left, – that is to say, those who were possessed by demons and with wild shouts, obscenities and blasphemies, which were not of themselves but of evil spirits, created disturbance during holy moments when there should be absolute quiet. All of these would leave, then the door into the main church was shut; only the faithful remained inside.

---

* Translator's note: In traditional Orthodox countries the sermon immediately follows the Gospel reading, and is an explanation of it.

After this historical information about the life of the early church, let us continue with the explanation of the Divine Liturgy.

"Again and many times we fall down before Thee and pray to Thee, in Thy goodness and love for mankind, to regard our supplications, and cleanse our souls and bodies from all defilement of flesh and of spirit, and grant that we may stand without guilt or condemnation before Thy holy altar. And upon these also who pray with us, O God, bestow increase of life and faith and spiritual insight. Give them always to worship Thee in fear and love, to share without guilt or condemnation in Thy holy mystery, and to be made worthy of Thy heavenly kingdom."

In this prayer we ask God to cleanse our souls and bodies "from all defilement of flesh and spirit." But what is this defilement? We will explain it in this homily.

There was a time, my beloved, when man was pure, clean from sin. For it is sin which infects the body and soul, making man unclean before God. According to the Bible, there was a time when the first man lived in paradise, having a pure heart and enjoying the blessings of natural creation (air, water, fruits of the trees), which also being virginal, were free from every infection. Everything was pure. But when man broke God's commandment and sinned, then sin, like an invisible microbe, attacked the entire spiritual and bodily organization of man and started the horrible pollution.

First the soul was infected; it was infected by pride and egotism. This infection spread, attacking man's body, and the body became the instrument of the soul in various sins. Yes, the body became the instrument of sin. Because from the soul that is infected and becomes filled with corruption the body takes its orders and executes them. The tongue speaks lies, gossip, slanders, calumnies, filth; it bears false witness and blasphemes God. The eyes see shameful spectacles. The ears hear words of unbelief and corruption with pleasure. The hands steal and kill. The legs run to the centers of debauchery and corruption. And in general, all the members of Man's body work for sin, and become infected by it. Prostitution, adultery, lewdness and other sins which man feels ashamed to even mention, infect his body very deeply.

St. John Chrysostom observes that he who commits carnal sins feels that his body is dirty and wants to wash himself immediately with plenty of water to be cleaned from the infection. The infection, however, is much deeper. A thousand baths and showers, and thousands of waterfalls can not purify man from the infection of carnal sins. This infection has progressed into the very least of the fibers and cells of his body. And the source, as we said, from which all this corporal infection comes is the soul. The soul is the one which becomes infected and corrupted first; it then imparts its infection everywhere.

The Soul is capable of sinning without the body's cooperation. It sins with evil wishes and cunning thoughts; it sins internally. In the secret and unseen depths of the inner world, it sins where man's eye can not see.

My God, how much is man infected; how much is he corrupted! He is in the church; he hears psalmodies, the Gospel and the sermon. He watches the celebration of the awesome mysteries. One would think that he would be in heaven. But if he is not careful, during this sacred time, his thoughts will slide away and go to persons and things of sin. The body which is in the church remains clean, but not the soul; it infects itself.

This is the "defilement of flesh and spirit" which St. Paul the Apostle admonishes us to escape by saying: "Let us cleanse ourselves from all filthiness of the flesh and spirit perfecting holiness in fear of God" (2 Cor. 7:1). The priest asks God to purify him and the faithful from this infection of body and soul. And being clean in body and soul to participate in the Holy Mysteries, to be made worthy to enter into the heavenly kingdom where none of the unclean are permitted.

Dearly beloved! Nowadays a big discussion is taking place in radio, television and in the newspapers about environmental pollution. The nations are all taking severe measures against this pollution, because they fear that the day will come when even the water and the air will be poison, and mankind will be destroyed.

Therefore, severe measures are taken against pollution. But as for the other pollution, the moral and religious; − not a word, no concern at all. Every day, radio and television pollute ears and eyes. And everything is cotributing to the progress of this pollution; mankind will become Sodom and Gomorrah, a filthy, unclean society, the end of which will be pitiful.

For that reason this prayer of the Church has great importance; we use it to pray to God to clean us "from every defilement of flesh and spirit."

CHRIST THE PANTOCRATOR

II

THE CHERUBIC HYMN
AND THE
GREAT ENTRANCE

A HORNET'S NEST

The Divine Liturgy, dearly beloved, is a holy drama: it is a representation of all the mystical, saving works of God. He who follows the Divine Liturgy from beginning to end attentively and with holy compunction, hears and sees marvelous things. From the darkness of the ancient world he hears gladsome voices: "Men, do not despair! The Redeemer of the world will come. The darkness will disperse and the sun, Christ, will rise." He sees the star of Bethlehem and hears of the angels: "Glory to Thee, Who hath shown forth the light." He sees the cave in the holy prothesis*, and Christ advancing towards the Jordan River to be baptized by St. John, marking the beginning of His public life. He hears preaching divine words, calling mankind to repentance and preparing the Apostles for the establishment of His kingdom.

The Christian, until the Gospel reading, sees, hears and marvels at these things in the Divine Liturgy. However, in the second part, in what is called the Liturgy of the Faithful, that which he shall see and hear and be made joyful by is far superior and more wondrous. Until the reading of the Gospel, Christ is like a teacher. Afterwards, He comes like a high priest in order to offer His

---

* Translator's note: The prothesis is the name of the service which we call the offertory, performed at the small altar, and is also the name of the small altar itself, found to the left of the main altar, which represents the cave of Christ's birth. An icon of the Nativity is traditionally present there.

blood for the life and salvation of the world. This is why the Christian who is getting ready to participate in the second part of the Divine Liturgy must become more attentive and have greater compunction. "Wisdom!" is the warning repeatedly heard at the beginning of the second part of the Divine Liturgy.

After the two moving prayers recited before the Great Entrance, and after the exclamation of the priest: "For being always guarded by Thy Power, to Thee we ascribe glory, to the Father, and to the Son and to the Holy Spirit, now and forever, and from all ages to all ages," the cantor chants the Cherubic Hymn. This is chanted in all the Divine Liturgies except a very few, and is as follows: "We who mystically represent the Cherubim sing the Thrice-holy Hymn to the life-giving Trinity. Let us put away all worldly care, so that we may receive the King of All. Invisibly escorted by the Angelic Orders. Alleluia, alleluia, alleluia."

In this hour, the Hymn says, when we are getting ready to receive the King of All like the angels and archangels in attendance, let us be very careful. Not only our body must be present, but more especially, our soul. All our thoughts must be directed towards Christ. We must not allow any other thought to disturb us.

We must pay attention to our Church's strong admonition: "Let us put away all worldly care."

To understand what this means, I will give an example from contemporary life.

There was a television set in a home. It was evening, the time for a program. Without asking their parents, the children turned on the T.V. and from that time on they glued their eyes to the set. Unfortunate children; they were expecting to be taught and educated by television! Two adults, however, sat down near them, and paying attention to the program were conversing together on a variety of topics. This conversation bothered the children because they could not hear clearly what the television was saying. One of the children became especially vexed, and with screams and threats demanded that the adult men stop speaking, so they could watch the television properly. They wanted complete silence in the television room. Everyone's eyes, their ears, and their brains should be glued to the set.

The same thing is happening with radio. When it is time to announce some important information concerning everyone, then all become silent before the radio; no one is permitted to speak.

What do we want to say with these two examples? That these things which we see and hear on television and radio, when we want absolute silence, are insignificant "rubbish" compared to those things which we see and hear in the Divine Liturgy. Yes, the Divine Liturgy is like a radio station from heaven, on which the voice of God is heard. It is like a television picture of heaven, in which the sweet face of our Lord Jesus Christ is seen. If we believe that Christ Himself speaks, appears and communicates through the Divine Liturgy, then it is necessary that all our attention be directed towards it. Everything inside ourself must be silent; only Christ must be heard and seen.

But, we ask, does this happen? Are our thoughts with Christ at the time when the Cherubic hymn is chanted? Unfortunately, that is the time our thoughts leave and go to different persons and things. At this time, a curious spiritual phenomenon can be observed, which shows how satan tries to detach our hearts from Christ. A variety of mundane thoughts occur. One person thinks about his wife. Another thinks about his children. A third thinks about his store. A fourth thinks about the chores he has to do. And others think of the vicissitudes of life. In there, inside the sacred hall of the church, man seeks to solve the problems which bother him. The cantor chants "we who mystically represent the Cherubim" and the thoughts of man wander outside the church. What a pity! The entire week has 168 hours, and unfortunately, man cannot and does not want to dedicate himself to Christ for even one.

O mundane thoughts, O cares of life! You will not leave us even during the hour of the Divine Liturgy. You continue to bother us even then! You surround us like hornets; you sting and bother us. But as they torch and burn the nest which bothers the travelers, freeing the wayfarers from its troublesome presence, so we must find a way to remove from our consciousness these vain thoughts which bother us and will not leave us un-distracted to follow the Divine Liturgy. We must destroy them and burn their nests.

Fire is needed, a burning love for Christ. Because when this kind of fire is kindled in the heart, then during the time of the Divine Liturgy no mundane thoughts and cares will have any place there. The person of our beloved Christ will attract us so much that we will not have eyes and ears to see and hear anything else but Him. And that way we will fulfill the admonition of the Church: "Let us put away all worldly cares, so that we may receive the King of All."

THE KING OF ALL

The Cherubic Hymn, dearly beloved, is the work of a pious emperor of Byzantium. It calls us, after we put away "all worldly cares," to receive the King of all. In this homily we will speak about the King of all and His reception.

And first, who is the King of all? If we take a look at the globe where we live, we will see that the earth is divided politically into various nations, with the form of government differing in each. There are various forms of government. In spite of the many differences in government, all nations, from the smallest to the largest, have someone at the top of the administration, who, depending on the form of government, is called king, president, commander-in-chief, secretary-general.... Regardless of the name which the highest leader might have, he never ceases to be that person whom all consider as the topmost power. He is the expression, the symbol of every nation.

The person who holds the highest degree of authority of the nation enjoys special honors. And whoever dares to insult or show disrespect to the person of the topmost leader, is punished by severe penalties; in totalitarian regimes he is punished by death.

Whenever the top leader of the nation leaves his place or presidential mansion to tour the cities and towns, the local authorities prepare a grand reception.

They call the people to come out and welcome him. Cities are decorated with flags. The army is lined up. Cheers, bouquets, addresses, dances in public squares, receptions and many other expressions take place, in order that the people might show their feelings of love and respect towards the highest authority.

History, old and new, mentions many receptions that the people have made for their earthly leaders. Most of these receptions were compulsory. The crowds were gathered, and cheered them by command. They could not do any differently. However, there were cases when the people received remarkable persons who had offered many great services to the people, and thus their reception in most such instances was profound and spontaneous.

All these, however, which have taken and take place here on earth regarding the great and powerful persons who hold the highest offices, are like a shadow of another reception, a spiritual reception which the souls must perform for the One Who is the real, the incomparable authority of the entire world. This leader did not receive and hold His authority by force and slaughter, or through lies, fraud and exploitation. His authority is spiritual, holy. He Himself is the source of His authority, because He is not a simple man with imperfections and defects, but is God. He is the God-man; He is our Lord Jesus Christ. He is, as the Cherubic Hymn chants, the King of all.

Who, of the worldly leaders can be compared, even remotely, with His holy Person? Or which form of government, regardless of how perfect it might seem, can compare with His Kingdom? Oh the leaders of the earth! Whatever name they may have, if they would have before themselves as an example Christ, the King of all, to be inspired and directed by Him and to serve the people with love and self-denial, the world would be different. But, unfortunately, now all the people groan and suffer more in some places and in others less, under imperfect political systems, all of which without exception are based on force, weapons and deception, and with only the percent of oppression differing from state to state. Therefore, on this bloodied land the prayer of Christians is heard: "Thy Kingdom Come" (Matt. 6:10). The world is far away, very far away, from that summit which is called the Kingdom of Christ.

Christ, the King of all, came here to earth. Indeed, He came without the external and vain characteristics of the political rulers of the earth, without clubs and knives, without force and exploitation, without lies and deceits. He came so humbly that the people did not recognize Him. And when Christ declared before Pilate that He was King of the Kingdom very different from the kingdom of the world, and the soldiers derisively dressed Him in a royal mantle, everyone mocked Him. "We do not have any king except Caesar of Rome," they shouted. "We don't have any other king and neither do we recognize. . . ." What a world! They were heavily taxed, they suffered and were tortured by the Caesars of Rome, and yet they wanted them and not Christ. They welcomed and worshipped them and not Christ, the King of justice and love. And the world continues to exhibit this wretched behavior, living under various political systems, which change every so often, with the hope that it shall find joy and happiness. But the source of joy and happiness is Christ, the King of all.

Every time there is a Divine Liturgy and the Cherubic Hymn is chanted, Christ comes in the humble form of bread and wine. He comes to offer His sacrifice form of bread and wine. He comes to offer His sacrifice for the salvation of the world. He comes. Yes! The King of all comes. And we the Christians are called to receive Him: to hasten to the church, to stand with reverence, and with feelings of deep gatitude, to receive Him when the priest, holding the precious gifts, comes out through the northern door of the sanctuary.

We cannot imagine with what deep contrition the Great Entrance was made in the ancient Church. And especially in the magnificent church of Haghia Sophia (Holy Wisdom) at Constantinople; it was very moving for someone to see the king, together with the highest officials, waiting outside the northern door of the sanctuary, in order to escort the celebrants of the Most High to the center of the church, where the holy procession used to stop, in order that the special supplications could be offered.

Then. . . . But now? Out of a hundred Christians, not even three go to church to receive Christ. And those three who go to church do not attend with the proper piety. But if on Sunday, when the Divine Liturgy is being celebrated, and the choir chants the Cherubic Hymn, if at that time some official comes to the city, then all go to welcome him with flags and banners, while only the priest and a very few Christians remain in the church.

The Church, with the Cherubic Hymn invites us: "Let us receive the King of all." While the world with its radios and televisions invites the people: "Let us receive the king, the president of the republic, or the prime minister or the minister. . . ."

How terrible for us! We honor the worldly authorities, but the King of all, Christ, we do not honor as we should. And not only do we not honor Him, but we blaspheme Him. Are we Christians?

THE PRAYER OF THE CHERUBIC HYMN

When the Cherubic Hymn, dearly beloved, is chanted, the priest stands before the Holy Table and reads the following prayer:

"None is worthy, among them that are enslaved by carnal desires and pleasures, to approach or come near or minister before Thee, the King of Glory; for Thy Service is great and fearful even to the Heavenly Powers. Yet since, through Thine ineffable and immeasurable compassion, Thou hast without change or differentiation become man and taken the title of our High Priest, as Lord of All, Thou hast committed to us the celebration of this rite and of the Bloodless Sacrifice. For Thou, O Lord our God, alone dost govern all things in heaven and in earth, Thou Who sittest upon the throne of the Cherubim and art Lord of the Seraphim and King of Israel, Who only art Holy and restest among Thy Saints. To Thee I persistently call, for Thou alone art righteous and ready to hear. Look upon me Thy sinful and unprofitable servant and purify my soul and heart from an evil conscience; enable me by the power of Thy Holy Spirit, girt with the grace of the Priesthood to stand at this Thy Holy Table and to consecrate Thy Holy and Spotless Body and Thy Precious Blood. For to Thee I come near, bowing down my neck, and Thee I beseech. Turn not away Thy Face from me, neither reject me from among Thy children, but consider me worthy, so that these Gifts may be brought near to Thee by me, Thy sinful and unworthy servant. For Thou art the Offerer and the Offered, the Acceptor and the Distributed, Christ our God, and to Thee we ascribe glory, with Thine Eternal Father and Thy most holy, righteous and life-giving Spirit, now and forever and from all Ages to all Ages. Amen."

This prayer of the Cherubic Hymn is one of the most inspired and moving prayers of the Divine Liturgy. Pious celebrants of the Most High at the time when they read it become filled with so much emotion, that they shed tears and their sobbings won't let them finish this superb prayer. How great is Christ, and how small and wretched is man! The greatness of Christ and the wretchedness of man, who dares to approach the holy altar and offer the Holy Mystery – this prayer emphasizes these two things.

Christ! O Christ, Thou art the Master of all. Thou dost govern, Thou dost command all that is heavenly, all that is earthly. Thou art Lord of the angels and archangels, of the Cherubim and the Seraphim. Thou alone art holy. Thou dost find gladness and Thou dost rest there where holiness is. Thou didst come from the heights of heaven here to earth. Thou didst come out of love for wretched man. A love which in the language of man cannot be expressed, and there is no measure to measure. Thy love is an endless ocean.

The priest. O Christ, what am I who ministers? I am thine unprofitable and worthless servant, who, even if I had kept all thy commandments, even so I am not worthy to gaze upon the height of Thy Majesty. It is a great and frightening thing for someone to serve Thee. With what hands can I touch Thee the Undefiled? With what tongue can I hymn and celebrate the sacred ceremony? I am afraid, Thou might reject me. Full of fear and reverence, Christ, I bend down, I worship Thee and beseech Thee. . . .

The priest must feel always his unworthiness, especially during the time when he is celebrating and offering the Highest Mystery. He himself should not be in his place, nor any other man, regardless of how perfect he is, but one of the angels and archangels of the heavenly world. And this could be done. Namely, every time when a Liturgy is about to be celebrated, an angel could come down from heaven, come here to earth, and celebrate the Holy Mystery. Nothing is impossible to God. Has not God sent angels many times here to earth to execute His commandments and serve the people? It would be possible for the angels and archangels to be entrusted with such a task.

What an astonishing phenomenon it would be, if upon entering the church we were to see an angel celebrating at the Holy Sanctuary! But this task, which angels and archangels would tremble to perform, has been entrusted to priests. Christ gave them the power to conduct the holy mysteries. St. John Chrysostom says that if we hypothesize that this spiritual power to remit sins and in general to perform the mysteries were given to the angels, because the angels have no conception of sin and of the temptations which people experience, they would be unable fully to understand and feel the human tragedy; likewise the people would come into contact with angels with great difficulty and reservations. But the priest, himself a sinful man who every day confronts temptations and fights the mighty fight against sin, sees on top of all that the weakness of people. He hears with great sympathy, as a fellow-sufferer, the sins of his fellow man, and is ready to give absolution to those who believe and sincerely repent.

Therefore let us thank Christ, because among the other benevolent acts towards mankind, he gave to men, to the priests, the spiritual power to forgive sins and to celebrate the mysteries in general.

The priest as a man may not be rich and powerful, wise and learned, one who impresses worldly people; he may be humble and disdained. However, from the moment when he receives and wears, as the prayer says, "the grace of ordination," he receives authority which is higher than any other. For even the most powerful and rich and learned person, as a sinner, needs to have his sins forgiven. And only the priest can give this absolution in the name of Jesus Christ. Having this kind of spiritual authority, he is above kings. He is superior to the angels and archangels, because God did not give to any of them this authority to forgive sins.

These things indeed, which we write here about the priests, are spiritual matters, and only he who believes understands and feels them. And when he sees a priest, he honors him as he should, because the priest has spiritual power, as a representative of Christ on earth. St. Cosmas the Aitolian used to say: "If you, my child, meet on your path both a priest and an Angel, first you must greet the priest and then the Angel, because the priest who performs and celebrates is superior to the Angels and Archangels."

Today, unfortunately, in an age of anarchy, unbelief and corruption, the priests of the Most High are not honored, and the majority of them are not even aware of the highness of their office.

May the Holy Spirit enlighten us, so that indeed the priests might feel Whose soldiers they are, and the people might not despise and disparage them, but might honor them like the angels of the Lord, the Creator of all.

THE INCENSE

After the prayer of the Cherubic Hymn, which we have explained in our previous homily, the celebrant priest takes the censor, and while saying the 50th Psalm in a low voice, censes the main altar and the prothesis. (Transl. note: The small altar, the preparation table on the north side of the Holy Bema.) He then comes out through the Beautiful Gate, and from there, censes in order the icons of Christ, the Most Holy Theotokos, John the Forerunner, and the patron saint of the church. Next he turns towards the congregation and censes all the people, men, women and children. But what is the meaning of this censing?

Even though we have spoken about incense previously, we will say a few more words about it.

Our Church uses incense often, and Christians should have an idea about its meaning and purpose, because no service takes place in the Church without it. The incense which burned in the holy churches is made of olibanum (frankincense) mixed with other aromatic essences. The pure incense, to put it another way, is the tear of a tree which is found in places of the East, in Lebanon and Arabia. As we here in Greece tap the pine tree for resin, in the same way the inhabitants of these countries tap the body of the incense tree, and from it drops a liquid like milk, pale yellow in color. This liquid thickens, they collect it and it becomes incense, which when burned on charcoal smells sweet.

As a certain philosopher says, dearly beloved, we are trees, heavenly trees. God plants us here on earth in order to produce fruits, to spread the aroma of faith and virtue, like the incense tree. But just as this tree must be cut in order to produce the choice product, incense, so we must pass through pain and sorrow, which like a knife incises our internal world, causing tears of true repentance and a return to God to come out from the depths of our hearts.

The incised trees cry. And also Christians cry, who in this world taste sorrows, difficulties and sufferings and feel their sinfulness. Trees do not produce incense without incisement; people do not produce the aroma of virtue without pains and sufferings. As the Holy Spirit says through the mouth of the Apostles Paul and Barnabas, "We must pass through many troubles to enter the Kingdom of God" (Acts 14:22).

Incense, as we see in the Old Testament, was used in divine worship. With it the archpriest and the priests censed the people in the tabernacle of the Witness and the Temple of Solomon. And their incense had meaning; prayers must be performed as God wants, because only such prayers are acceptable to Him. And, as the smoke of the incense rises up, in the same way the prayers of pious people rise up towards heaven. The prophet King David says: "Let my prayer be set forth as incense before Thee, the lifting up of my hands as an evening sacrifice" (Psalm 140:2, (141:2)).

In the New Testament we see that Zacharias, the Father of John the Forerunner, when his turn of service came in the temple of God and all the people were praying, while he was censing the holy sanctuary, saw an angel of the Lord standing to the right of the altar. When

Zacharias saw him he was frightened. But the angel calmed him and said to him: "Be not afraid; God has heard your prayer and your wife Elizabeth will bear you a son, and you shall name him John (Luke 1:8-13).

The priest, the pious priest Zacharias, saw an angel when he was censing. One of the great fathers and teachers of the Church, St. Ambrose, commenting on this exceptional event says: "May an angel be present when we too cense the holy sanctuary." Yes, may an angel be present. As John the Evangelist saw in his Revelation. When he opened the seventh seal, an angel came and stayed on the holy sanctuary holding a golden censor. And much incense was given to the angel. This incense was the prayers and petitions of the saints. And the angel took the censor and filled it with fire from the sanctuary, and the incense burned (Rev. 8:3-4).

Incense, therefore, is a symbol of the prayers of the Christians. The archpriest or the priest who censes, is gathering, in a way, the prayers from all the worshippers. It is a striking exhortation for prayer. It is like saying to them: Christians, pray and send your silent prayers to the Heavenly Father. All united together will perform the miracle. They will attract the great grace of God. . . . And because incense has this kind of meaning, for this reason, when the celebrant priest censes, the congregation must rise from their seats, step away from the stalls (stasidia) and make a bow. This is an answer to the priest's invitation for prayer.

O eyes, drop tears, like the incense trees. O hearts of sinners, be humble and pray to God.

There is also another meaning given to incense by a newer ecclesiastical writer of blessed memory, Konstantinos Kallinikos. He composed a beautiful poem dedicated to incense. He says in this poem: Black coal am I, the sinful man. Black like the coal. Black from my many sins. Indifferent, frosty, cold. I the sinner, and cold. The Church has the fire of heaven. She inflames souls and makes them shine with divine radiance, to spread their aroma, and to send prayers to heaven.

If we consider this explanation, the censer symbolizes the temple, the church. That is why it is formed like a church. The censer is held with four thin chains, which, as some commentators say, symbolize the four Evangelists, who are painted at the four pendentives of the dome. And the top piece of the censer is shaped like a dome.

Now, my Christians, that you have heard the meaning of the incense and censer, I believe that at the time when the celebrant priest of the Most High perfumes you with incense, you will not stand indifferent, but you will direct silent prayers to God from the bottom of your heart: Prayers for your spiritual progress, prayers for the members of your family, prayers for your relatives, for the priests, for the teachers, prayers for the world.

And these prayers will rise in the air like fragrant incense. And you pious women must have a censer next to the iconostasis, perfume your home with incense and with your warm prayers make your home a church. For where there is incense, where there is prayer, the devil can not stay.

THE PSALM OF REPENTANCE

Dearly beloved, while the priest is censing the holy altar, the icons, and all the people, he says the 50th psalm, the: "Have mercy on me, O God, according to Thy great mercy. . . ." Because this psalm is said not only during this sacred moment of the Divine Liturgy, but during other holy services of our Church as well, and is one of the most important psalms, the psalm of repentance, we will devote two homilies to it.

First of all let us see the historical background of this psalm. The author of this psalm is David. He was not born in palaces. He was not the child of a king or some other rich or powerful man. He was a poor boy. His father, Jesse, had many children, and lived out of doors. He had eight male children. David was the youngest, and grazed his father's sheep. However, this youngest son of Jesse the Bethlehemite was a charming young man. Divine providence chose him to become the king of Israel; the prophet Samuel by God's order went and found him and anointed him King. While he was still a youth, he showed marvelous signs of his abilities. He fought and killed a lion that came to destroy his flock. Then he fought and defeated an enormous giant, the idolator Goliath, who had challenged all the Israelites to single combat with him, and no one dared. David, however, dared, and with his sling he hit and killed Goliath, and delivered the Israelite nation from its shame. For this feat of his he was glorified like a national hero. They received him in the palaces, and after the death of Saul he was proclaimed king. And like a king he organized the army and marched against the many enemies of Israel. He defeated them and greatly extended his country's borders. Never before had Israel reached such glory as in the days of King David.

Who would imagine that this shepherd boy, who grazed his poor father's sheep, would become the most famous king? Therefore we must not despise any man, regardless of how insignificant he might be. The future is unknown; only God knows it.

But great deeds are often followed by failings and humiliations. This same David who killed the lion in the desert, who defeated the giant Goliath, who defeated so many enemies and was glorified as a national hero and reached great heights, this victor over beast and man, was himself defeated.

David was defeated? Yes, he was defeated. By whom? By his own self. How? Holy Writ narrates the following in the Book 2 Samuel 11. One day while he was walking on the roof terrace of the palace he spied a naked woman taking her bath in a neighboring home. Her name was Bathsheba. Her beauty defeated him. That quick look sparked a furnace of shameful passion in his heart. Oh how dangerous it is to see the bodies of people who walk almost naked in the streets and squares, to baths in mixed company at the sea! Even David fell, and yet you have so much trust in yourself that you think that you are in no danger from the shameful spectacles of our age?

David, the most glorious king of Israel fell. And he fell into two horrible sins. Bathsheba was not single, she was married. Her husband, Uriah, was an excellent

officer of Israel, and he was at the front. David man-
aged it so that he was sent to the most dangerous line,
and while fighting against the enemies of his country
he was killed. In this way, David took Bathsheba into
the palace as his wife. He committed two mortal sins,
adultery and murder.

While David had committed these two horrible sins,
he had not consciousness of what he had done. He lived in the palace and amused himself as if nothing was
wrong. He slept in the heavy sleep of sin. But he woke
from that heavy sleep. Who brought him to consciousness and led him to ask for the mercy of God? The
prophet Nathan. While all those close to the king, the
courtiers and officials, did not dare say anything to the
king, he dared go up to the palace. Using a parable he
succeeded in awakening his conscience and making
David cry out: "I have sinned" (2 Samuel 12).

Preaching was the thing which woke David's conscience, the preaching which Nathan preached in the
palace in an educational kind of way. Without this
preaching David would not have awakened from the
heavy sleep of sin. The preaching was the alarm clock.
Let them hear who hate and dislike sermons and do not
want the word of God heard anywhere. God uses many
means to make people repent and return to Him. But
His most powerful means is His word. A Church without
preaching will become a dead Church. It will consist of
people who sin like David, and have no Nathan to wake
them up.

After Nathan's preaching David repented. He
evinced a repentance that man seldom shows in this sinful world. His repentance was a deep repentance, a
sincere repentance, which is moving. During the night,

while everyone slept, David cried. His eyes became like fountains; he shed continuous tears. He soaked the mattress of his bed with them. And from the depths of his aching, pained heart, a warm prayer to God arose.

He beseeched God to forgive him his sins. The words of this prayer are the 50th psalm. This psalm should become our prayer too. For we, some more some less, are sinners too. And may God give us a tear from the tears that King David shed like rivers when he became conscious of his sinfulness.

Many teachers and preachers of the Holy Gospel have commented on the 50th psalm, which is one of the most beautiful poems that man has written. Volumes have been written explaining its meaning. In the next homily, with God's help, we will try to give you an idea about this psalm.

"THY GREAT MERCY"

The 50th psalm, the famous psalm of repentance, dearly beloved, is a collection of 21 poetic verses, each one of which is like a diamond; it is a collection of brilliants. Let us look at the first verse which is as follows: "Have mercy on me, O God, according to Thy great mercy; and according to the multitude of Thy compassions blot out my transgression." Thus starts the psalm.

If somene hears this verse and has no knowledge of the historical background of the psalm, he may suppose that some hungry beggar is knocking at the door of a rich man asking for help. But the one who is asking for help here is not some poor abandoned man. He is the most glorious king of Israel. In spite of it, this king appears, here in the first verse, like a wretched beggar asking for help. Is not this offensive, and is this not a diminution and disgrace of man? Those who continuously praise man consider such expressions of the Holy Bible as suitable for the slaves of ancient times. But certainly this is not so. A serious investigation concerning mankind will show that man, in spite of his astonishing progress in the technical and scientific fields, in reality is an unhappy being, who suffers and groans even though he is swimming in a richness of material things. A certain vacuum exists inside him. The machines he invented to make his life easier and happier have subjugated him and made him their slave. Like wild tyrants they seek to crush and destroy him. From master man has become a servant. A servant, a slave serving in a technocratic civilization which not only has not liberated him from human passions and evils, but has added its own oppressive weight; and the apparently free man in reality is a slave worse off than those of the ancient world. In the chaos of this technocratic civilization man feels the need of deliverance from the internal slavery of the passions, and from the external slavery of the modern world. And if at one time in the old days man sought God's mercy, he has greater need today, in the 20th century, which with machines makes people servants and slaves who tremble and fall down and worship contemporary idols.

The poet asks God's mercy. But in this verse he is not asking simply for mercy, but for the great mercy. A distinction is made between small and great. Small is called the mercy which in essence is not small, but is small in comparison with the other, the great mercy.

Let us explain ourselves clearly. Small mercy concerns the practical goods which the omnipotent and most gracious God gives us. For example, the rain which falls and moistens the fields and makes the earth bloom and the plants and trees to bear fruits and the markets to fill up with choice produce, is a manifestation of God's love; it is the mercy of God. The air, refreshing and vivifying, which the whole planet and all mankind breathes, that too is a demonstration of God's mercy. The rays of the sun, which come from so far a distance to illuminate and warm the earth, is another manifestation of God's mercy. And these three blessings, to limit ourselves only to these, are given freely to all people without exception. As Christ says, the heavenly Father "maketh his sun to rise on the evil and on the good, and sendeth rain on the just and on the unjust" (Matt. 5:45).

God, therefore, is merciful to the world. He shows mercy every day. What am I saying? Every hour. What am I saying? Every moment. For if the springs dry up, if the wind stops blowing, if the oxygen ends, if the sun darkens and goes out, who can live on this planet? God is merciful therefore to all of us, even to those unbelievers who, from an endless egotism, even though they receive all the blessings of divine creation, do not feel the need to express their gratitude to God.

But besides the material blessings which the heavenly Father God scatters throughout the whole world, there is another blessing which is incomparably greater than all the rest of the goods of this world. What is this blessing? Let us again bring to mind David, who is the author of the psalm. What did we say? David was not poor. He was not in need; he was rich in material goods. He had money, pleasures, amusements and great glory. If someone was passing by the palace, he would bless him and say: Here is a happy man. He has everything. . . . This man, however, was not happy. Because he had committed two horrible crimes and the hour came when his conscience was crying out: "You are a sinner. You find yourself separated from and at war with God, for you despised His holy will. And if God wants to judge you for your offense against His divine commandments, what will you say in apology? God honored you, favored you. He protected you from various dangers; you should be thankful to Him and show your gratitude with absolute obedience and obey His authority."

Oh man! Even if you have a royal crown on your head and all men bow down and pay homage to you, you are a sinner. The courts of men cannot judge you. But the Court of God?. . . How are you going to escape divine judgement?

My God! David cries out, the repentant sinner cries out. I feel my guilt. I see the deep corruption of my heart. My roots are sinful. Sinful are the parents who gave me birth. They are descendants of Adam and Eve. From there originates the inclination and tendency towards sin. I do not want to sin. But my will is very small and weak. I do that which I do. I fall into sin. However, I am not senseless and indifferent. A spark burns inside me. A voice does not stop censuring me as an offender of the divine law. I have nothing to offer you, O Lord, but a pitiful and unclean heart. O Lord, I ask for Thy mercy, Thy great mercy. . . .

This great mercy is the forgiveness of sins. It is a forgiveness which derives only through Christ's sacrifice on the cross. Yes! Christ's Blood is the endless ocean of God's mercy and compassion. He washes, cleans and regenerates the sinner. The voice of the Crucified One "Courage my son! Thy sins are forgiven" (Matt. 9:2), continues to be heard through the father confessors and is an answer of heaven to the sinner, who by having a broken and repentant heart falls down and worships the Redeemer of the world, saying the prayer of repentance: "Have mercy on me, O God, according to Thy great mercy; and according to the multitude of Thy compassions blot out my transgressions."

THE PRECIOUS GIFTS

The celebrant priest, after censing the holy altar table, the prothesis (the small preparation altar table), the holy icons and the people, with a slight bow having asked for forgiveness from the people saying: "Those who hate and do wrong to us, O God, forgive," goes to the holy prothesis. The precious gifts are there which we must now bring from the prothesis to the holy altar table. This transfer, as we have said, is called the Great Entrance. We spoke about the precious gifts previously. But here too, let us say a few words about them, having now as a helper the explanation of a famous mystic teacher of the Church, Nicholas Kavasilas, who interpreted the Divine Liturgy in a series of homilies.

In ancient times, before Christ, the Jews and even other people offered as sacrifices "the first-fruits" at the sacrificial altars which they had for the worship of God, the first that is to say and the best born and grown sheep, calves and crops of the earth. We Christians, instead of these, following the commandment of Christ, offer something greater. We offer bread and wine.

And these are greater because the fruit of this earth, as it falls from the trees, is feed for animals. But bread and wine are something different. In order for bread and wine to be made, man's cooperation is essential. Animals are not able to make bread; they eat the crops as they find them. But man plants, harvests, threshes, separates the crop, the wheat from the chaff, brings the wheat to the mill, makes flour, kneads the flour, bakes it, and it becomes bread. How much effort, how much labor, for the wheat to become bread! Certainly, the most important of all, the basis, is the wheat, the first and most necessary material. But if the heavens do not rain, what will the farmers harvest, what will the mills grind, and what will the bakers knead? Thus we can say that God gives it. But man's cooperation is needed for the preparation of bread.

And what we said about bread, we now say about wine, the other necessary ingredient for the performance of the mystery of the divine Eucharist. To become wine, grapes must be gathered at the right time, brought to the presses or the modern factories. From the machinery comes out and is collected the juice of the grapes and it becomes wine.

Also for your salvation, my dear Christian, your own cooperation is needed. God wants you to be saved and offers everything for your salvation. But you must want to and put forth effort, which, in comparison with what God gives as a basic blessing, is very small, it is a thousandth of it.

Bread and wine, material things, we offer as gifts to God. And God, Who is the giver of these blessings, will become also "the provider of reward, the righteous judge Who puts all things on the balance and weighs them." That is to say, God, Who gives us the bread and wine and commands us to offer them as gifts, the same provider and law-giver, is ready to return the spiritual, His infinitely superior gifts, which have a certain likeness and relationship to our own offerings. The Lord is accustomed to doing this, as we see in the Gospel.

To the rich man, whom He invited to sell his posses-
sions and give (the money) to the poor, He promised that
in place of that he would give him spiritual riches, the
Kingdom of Heaven. The rich man would have given
gravel, and would have received diamonds. To the
Apostles, whom He called to leave off fishing, He promised that instead of fishing for fish in the lake, they
would do another, greater kind of fishing: they would
become fishers of men. And in the Divine Liturgy, in
order to give us the real, the everlasting, the living, the
heavenly bread, which is He Himself, He calls upon us
to offer earthly bread.

The bread and wine which are on the holy prothesis
and are going to be transferred during the Great Entrance
to the holy altar, certainly are called precious gifts, being destined for the great mystery, but they are not yet
sanctified. That is to say, they have not yet changed into
the Body and Blood of Christ. This great miracle will
take place later. Only in the Presanctified Liturgy the
precious gifts which the priest transfers are not bread
and wine, but the precious body and the precious blood
of our Christ, because they have been presanctified in
another Liturgy. That is why in the Liturgy of the Presanctified, during the Great Entrance, the faithful kneel
and venerate: they are venerating Christ. It is not however the same in other Divine Liturgies.

However, because the bread and wine which are
transferred have been set apart and dedicated to Christ
with the prayers said at the prothesis, for this reason
Christians receive them with pious feelings. We are not,
as the heretics accuse us, bread-worshippers and wine-
worshippers; because we believe that, according to
Christ's words, these elements transferred by the priest

are changed (during the Liturgy) into the body and blood of Christ. Many persons, mostly because of lack of education, ignore what is said and takes place during the Divine Liturgy, and cannot make the distinction between the presented precious gifts and the body and blood of Christ, between the image and the reality.

The Great Entrance is made with a line-up and procession. With special magnificence it was made in the church of the Holy Wisdom in Constantinople. The Emperor, who was present in the church, left his designated place (his throne) before the Great Entrance, proceeded to and entered the Holy Sanctuary, put on a golden cloak, holding a cross in one hand and his sceptre in the other, and now as a sexton or an (altar) boy carried the censer and led in the Great Entrance. As a servant of the most great king Christ, the Emperor led the holy procession. To his left and right were one hundred noble young men with a battalion of soldiers. And behind them followed the deacons and priests carrying the precious gifts.

The Emperor, that is to say the highest official of the great Empire of Byzantium, considered it as the highest honor to serve as a sexton in the church during the Divine Liturgy. How things have changed now! Where is there today a high official of the state who deigns to carry the censer and to serve in the church during the frightening hour of the Divine Eucharist? Not only will you now find a high official, but not even a child can be found in some churches to carry the censer and the candle during the Great Entrance.

Other times, other customs. Our age is one of unbelief, atheism, and corruption. Unfortunately, the bad example comes from those who should be the first in devoutness.

THE GRATEFUL THIEF

In a previous homily, dearly beloved, we spoke about incense. The celebrant priest having censed, said the fiftieth psalm to himself, and asked for forgiveness, saying: "O God, forgive those who hate and do wrong to us." Then together with the deacon, if there is one, he goes to the prothesis, takes the fabric which covers the paten and the holy chalice with great reverence, the aer as it is called (literally: air or wind), and puts it on the shoulders of the deacon, saying this verse of David: "Lift up your hands unto the holies, and bless the Lord" (133,2 LXX-134,2 K.J.). Then the priest gives the paten to the deacon. The deacon holds it on his head with reverence; and the priest takes the holy chalice in his hands. Thus they come out through the northern door, proceed and come before the Beautiful Gate, while the congregation with their heads bowed in reverence welcome the precious gifts. Then the deacon says with a loud voice: "May the Lord, our God, remember us all in His Kingdom, now and ever, and unto ages of ages."

These words are a petition to Christ. They are taken from the prayer which the grateful thief, who was crucified to the right of Christ, said, "Remember me, Lord, when thou comest into thy kingdom" (Luke 23, 42). At that moment of the Divine Liturgy, we remember this grateful criminal and we repeat, through the deacon or the priest, his very moving and touching prayer. Thus the grateful thief appears in our minds and is presented as an example of faith and sincere repentence. Let us say a few words about this grateful thief.

All of us know from the Holy Gospels, that Pontius Pilate, the governor of Judea, made a great effort that Christ might not be condemned to death, as His fanatic enemies were asking. At that time in the prison, among other criminals, was a notorious one, Barabbas. Pilate having in his mind a custom which took place during the holy day of Passover, according to which the governor would spare the life of a condemned convict, whoever the people wanted, proposed to set Christ free. But the mob, which was made fanatical by the archpriests, the scribes, and the pharisees, cried out no! Instead of Christ the mob asked that Barabbas should be set free. Pilate retreated and signed the condemnation of Christ. Together with Him it was ordered that two thieves be executed.

Who were these two thieves? An old tradition preserves the name of one. Dysmas was the name of the thief crucified to the right of Christ.

We ask: Were these two thieves born criminals? We answer: No one, beloved, is born a criminal or a saint. He becomes one. We do not deny that the child may be born with a heavy heredity which he receives from his parents and may have the inclination and tendency towards crime. But in spite of the pressure his sinful nature exercises on man, he is still free to choose the good or the bad. When, however, the child is raised in a wretched family environment, when he sees and hears bad examples, the child mimicks them and becomes a thief, a gangster, a killer and criminal. For this reason those who commit different crimes and are convicted and imprisoned are not the only ones responsible for them, but many others are accomplices, who did not take care with their teaching and good example to prevent the evil. First of all the parents are responsible. Teachers are responsible. Responsible, also, is the whole society, in the midst of which a person lives and acts.

And for these two thieves, the society of the Jews of that time bore responsibility. They were not the only thieves in the community. No. Perhaps these were the lesser thieves and robbers. Others, with great and high and sacred offices, such as the archpriests of the Jewish people, in their way were robbing and stealing from the people, and made the temple, the house of God, a house of commerce and a den of thieves.

Perhaps close to the Praetorium were the jails, and the two thieves heard the wild voices of the people that Friday morning, demanding with such frenzy the death of Christ. But how could they imagine that many hours would not pass and the iron doors of the prison would open and the soldiers would take them to the place of execution together with Christ. With how much curiosity, I wonder, these two thieves looked at this condemned one. In Christ's face they did not see any cruelty. Peace and meekness were pictured on it.

And now the two thieves, with Christ between them, loaded with their crosses, climb with Him to terrible Golgotha. Many people accompany them. For these two no disapprobation takes place. Nó one curses them. Christ's enemies, however, even in this hour when he is walking to Golgotha, curse and mock Him. Unfortunately, the two thieves are no exception. Instead of expressing some kind of sympathy to their co-condemned, they were influenced by the general clamor and they too were insulting Him.

But Christ on the cross, before delivering up His spirit to the heavenly Father, did His miracle. Which one? One of the thieves, Dysmas, who was crucified at Christ's right side, started seeing things differently. A mystical ray from the Sun of righteousness illuminated his heart. He saw that Christ was not a common man, but someone who hides in Himself an unattainable moral grandeur. In these cruel hours of the crucifixion, when people lost control of themselves and cursed and swore, Christ not only did not curse or swear but blessed and prayed for His crucifiers. His words "Forgive them, Father; for they know not what they do" (Luke 23,34), touched the heart of that thief. He stops cursing and swearing, and undertakes Christ's defense, he rebukes the other thief, and if he were free he would fall before the feet of the Crucified-One and ask for His mercy. This, however, he cannot do; his body is tied. But his soul is free and flies to heavenly worlds and directs a prayer to the Savior Christ. It is a prayer which since then, and until today, and until the end of time will touch the souls of sinners and will become their own prayer: "Remember me, Lord, when Thou comest into Thy Kingdom" (Luke 23:42).

O my Brethren! Outside the church, while the Divine Liturgy is being celebrated, people are blaspheming Christ with the most vulgar words. Inside the church, a few souls are found. And these souls, when the Holies pass by, with great reverence mentally bow down before Christ, remember the grateful thief and say: "Remember me, Lord, when Thou comest into Thy kingdom."

Thus Christ's drama is continued until today. Others blaspheme Him, as did the thief at His left; others venerate and worship Him, as did the thief at His right.

SAINT JOHN CHRYSOSTOM

III

A NEW SET
OF PETITIONS

NEW PETITIONS

When the priest has finished the commemorations at the Great Entrance, he goes into the holy Sanctuary, reverently puts the paten and chalice on the Holy Table and covers them with the Aer. He then sends up to God a new series of petitions. These begin with the priest's invitation, "Let us complete our prayer to the Lord.' All together, there are ten petitions and they prepare the faithful spiritually to offer the Mystery of the holy Eucharist. Some of them have been mentioned before. The new petitions are:

1. "For the precious Gifts, here presented, let us pray to the Lord."

2. "For this whole day, that it may be perfect, holy, peaceful and sinless, let us ask of the Lord."

3. "For an Angel of peace, a faithful guide, a guardian of our souls and bodies, let us ask of the Lord."

4. "For things that are good and profitable to our souls and for peace of the world, let us ask of the Lord."

5. "That the rest of our life may be spent in peace and repentance, let us ask of the Lord."

6. "That the end of our life may be Christian, painless, blameless, and peaceful; that we may have a good defense before the fearful judgement Seat of Christ, let us ask of the Lord."

Let us examine the first two of these petitions in this homily.

With the words, "For the precious Gifts, here presented . . . ," our attention is brought to the precious Gifts. These are the same precious gifts we talked about in the last homily. Perhaps, though, someone who hears this petition may ask: "If the Gifts are precious, why do we need this petition?" Yes, they are precious – they have been pure since the Service of Preparation. But now they are on the holy Table and the great Mystery is about to take place. The bread will become Christ's Body and the wine will become Christ's Blood; and the priest calls everyone in the church to receive Communion, to pray.

Also, as a modern commentator on the holy Eucharist says, at this time when the precious Gifts are placed on the Table, we are being told to remember that our hearts must be clean of every evil and vengeful stain, as the Lord has said: "So, if you are about to offer your gift to God at the altar and there you remember that your brother has something against you, leave your gift there . . ." (Matt. 5:23-24). That is to say, unless you forgive your enemies, you should not offer gifts. Look at your gifts on the holy Table: Your hearts must be pure!

As for the next petition, "For this whole day, that it may be perfect, holy, peaceful and sinless . . . ," we should say the following:

Our most benevolent God has created everything in His wisdom, and has divided time into the twenty-four hours of day and night. Night is the time when man rests from his day's work. When the sun sets, the wild animals come out of their dens and, hungry, search for their food; and before the sun rises, they hide themselves again in their lairs. Unfortunately, there are some people who don't sleep at night. This is not because some duty forces them to stay up at night, as with medical doctors, sailors, soldiers, etc., but because they think night is a suitable time to do their dark deeds. How many people stay awake to visit night clubs, discotecs, casinos and to play cards? These people, living by night, have become like wild animals that come out at night to hunt, catch and tear their victims to pieces.

God appointed the day for man's work. As David says in the Vesper Psalm: "The sun ariseth, and they are gathered together, and they lay them down in their dens. But man shall go forth unto his work, and to his labour until the evening" (Psalm 103:24-25).

Day is the time to work, and you can see everybody, men and women (except for the sick, the old and the lazy), leaving for work in the morning. And during the day, they meet with dilemmas, snags and temptations stemming from many sources. We are not living in a society of angels and archangels; we are living in a society of men having faults and vices. And when we are forced to work together, we taste the bitterness of our fellow men's behavior. Even if no one bothers us, however, the evil within us does not stop bothering us, and the first chance we get, we ignite the flame of sin and get ourselves in trouble. And the devil lies in wait, ready to use every opportunity to plunge us into sin.

Temptation from within and around us has us encircled. As St. Anthony the Great once saw in a vision, the entire earth is filled with traps, and wherever we go or wherever we are, if we are not careful, we are in danger of falling into sin. Traps in the cities, traps in the towns, traps in the streets and squares, and even traps in deserts and monasteries, where you may think there are no temptations!

Every hour has its temptations, and as psychologists observe, as the day rolls by and noontime approaches, and as the pressures of work increase, one is apt to lose heart and say or do something unbecoming, improper and sinful. The published statistics show that most criminal acts occur around noontime. The Psalmist notes: "Thou shalt not be afraid . . . of the arrow that flieth by day . . . , nor of the mishap and demon of noonday" (Psalm 90:5-6).

What do we need to save ourselves from life's many temptations? First of all, we need attention. Let us pay attention to our thoughts, because every sin and crime starts there. If we stay alert and drive evil thoughts out of our minds, we will have the first victory over temptation. Because we are spiritually weak, however, temptation comes on us very strongly, and we need God's help. Whoever thinks he has a strong character and is invincible is in a position to commit even more horrible crimes. There are terrible times in our lives when we are completely destroyed spiritually, and divine grace saves only those who ask for it in humility.

Therefore, let us ask of God at the beginning of every day that it be "perfect, holy, peaceful and sinless."

"FOR AN ANGEL OF PEACE"

"For an angel of peace, a faithful guide, a guardian of our souls and bodies, let us ask of the Lord."

This petition is one of the ten petitions said immediately after the Great Entrance. With this petition we ask God to send an angel to guard our souls and bodies.

An angel? Unbelievers hearing this would ridicule Christians, who, in the twentieth century, believe in the existence of angels. An astronaut of an atheistic state once said, that when he flew in space, he did not so much as see an angel's wing! What foolishness! He was expecting to see an angel.... The area in which the atheist astronaut flew was very small, indeed, the smallest part of the endless universe. And even if he were able to fly through the entire universe in his rocket, he would not find an angel's wing. This is because an angel is not a material creature, to be seen by mortal eyes.

As to whether angels exist or not depends on an answer to a more basic question: Does God exist? Yes or no? If God does not exist, then neither do angels. The one who denies the existence of God, the Supreme Spirit, naturally denies the existence of lower spirits, the angels. Such a person accepts only material things and nothing else.

However, the person who accepts matter and nothing else cannot progress in his argument to answer those enormous questions which arise from his denial of the spirit. Let's mention the one problem that the atheist and materialist cannot solve: human thought, which is immaterial, something spiritual, which we cannot grasp or weigh on a scale. Where does it come from? From matter? A handful of dirt, a piece of metal does not have mind. Matter does not possess reason.

The materialist, who does not accept the creed "I believe in one God, the Father almighty . . .", is forced to believe in another dogma which presents much greater difficulties than those of the Christian doctrine. The unbeliever says: "I believe in omnipotent matter. . . ." How illogical is the Creed of materialists!

For the man who thinks rationally, and believes that there is God, Who created the world, the question as to whether angels exist or not finds a logical answer. Please follow our thought:

If we look at the universe, we see that is made up of countless parts, elements, atoms, which are combined in various ways and appear in a variety of forms. It comprises forms from the most simple to the most complex, from the smallest to the largest. First, we have the earth, the stones and metals. Next there are plants, the trees and forests. Then the insects, birds and animals. The highest of these creatures is man. Man is composite. He is body and soul. As a body, he belongs to the material world; as a soul, he belongs to the unseen spiritual world. And as certain as we are that man is a body, so sure we are that he is soul. Man is a compound of matter and spirit.

The question is raised: Could not God, Who created man as a link between the visible and invisible worlds also create beings having no body, but only spirit? He certainly could, and He did create such beings. These are angels.

The existence of angels, which reason does not reject, is confirmed in the word of God, Holy Scripture. Anyone who reads the Bible can see that angels and archangels are mentioned there many times. We shall mention two Scriptural passages:

"When the stars were made, all my angels praised me with a loud voice" (Job 38:7).

In this passage, the existence of angels is not only affirmed, but also the time of their creation. The angels and archangels existed before the heavens and the stars were made. Such a spectacle the heavens and shining stars presented, that the angels and archangels, seeing such a marvelous thing rise out of chaos, could not stand indifferent and apathetic, but were filled with admiration, and began praising and glorifying the omnipotent and all-wise God. Truly, one of the most convincing proofs of God's existence and His grandeur is the sight of the heavens at night.

The material world has stars, but the spiritual world has its stars as well. In the spiritual world, the angels shine like stars; and above the spiritual lights of the angels is the eternal and inaccessible light of the triune Deity, the Holy Trinity: Father, Son and Holy Spirit.

Another biblical passage which affirms the existence of the angelic world was spoken by our Lord Jesus Christ Himself. He who created both material and spiritual worlds, and who knows with all detail what moves and has being, Christ Himself said that everyone, even a person the world considers small and unimportant, is protected by the Father. The same angels who, by the command of our heavenly Father guard and protect the lowliest people of the earth, also surround God's throne and pray for those to whom they are assigned as guardians. Christ said we should be sure never to look down on the lowly people of earth. . . . Here are the very words of Christ: "See that you do not despise any of these little ones. Their angels in heaven, I tell you, are always in the presence of my Father in heaven" (Matt. 18:10).

What a comfort there is in the fact that we have someone next to us ready to protect and guard us!

Dear friends, a great painter once painted an angel, who with big white wings guards a small child as he crosses a dangerous river bridge. The child is in danger of slipping and falling into the river, but the angel protects him.

In order to keep this angel by our side as our guardian and protector, we have to be careful not to sin. It is because of this that the angel leaves us and laments. Yes! We sin and laugh, while angels cry and lament in heaven because we have fallen. Lord, have mercy on us!

"FOR THINGS THAT ARE GOOD AND PROFITABLE"

"For things that are good and profitable to our souls and for peace of the world, let us pray to the Lord."

Many people unacquainted with religion cite the words of this petition to lay claim to material benefits for themselves or for others. However, the true meaning of this excellent petition of the Church bears no resemblance to their interpretation. If a person is worldly-minded, his understanding of God's words will also be worldly. Unfortunately, worldly people also take other divine words of lofty meaning and use them in an improper or disrespectful way. God's word, true gems, are not appreciated by the materialist or atheist. Just as a pig can have no appreciation for diamonds, so the person who has a piggish soul (that is, whose soul always thinks materialistically), can find no value in spiritual things.

The materialistic concept of life is so strong, that it influences even religious people connected to the Church and who call upon God. What are we looking for? All those who have not been regenerated by the Holy Spirit and have never considered the value of a holy, spiritual life, but are influenced by the way the world thinks, are so influenced even in their prayers. When they light candles and vigil lamps before the holy icons, they pray to God and endeavor to use the saints as mediators to get things that are worldly, absurd and sinful.

Do you want to know what these people ask for? A man did his neighbor wrong and they go to court. The first prays to God to let him win the case. The wretch! He prays, wanting God, who hates injustice and loves righteousness, to be the partner, supporter and rewarder of his injustice. . . .

Another man or woman, falling into shameful love, goes to country chapels, lights candles and makes votive offerings to win the assistance of God's grace, so that their desire can be fulfilled. As if the pure and spotless religion of Christ will play the role of cheap panderer like the ones disreputable men use as go-betweens to achieve their sinful purposes. God, who hates prostitution and adultery, is called on to aid and become a partner in dishonorable doings. . . .

A third person, who suffered some injustice, harbors an irreconcilable hatred against the one who wronged him, and, not intending to forgive him, goes to Church and prays to God to punish the one who wronged him, filling his prayer with horrible curses. This person has forgotten that Christ on the Cross did not ask to punish or revenge His crucifiers, but asked His heavenly Father to forgive them. . . .

A fourth, who wants to get rich quick, buys a ticket and goes to church to ask the saints to help him win first prize. . . .

And there are many more who ask God for absurd and sinful things.

And because God does not fulfill their requests, they are scandalized. To such people, who want to make God a partner in their ignominy and foolishness, we say the same words that Christ said to His two disciples, James and John. Do you remember this incident? On the

evening before His passion, Christ was talking about the
terrible martyrdom He was about to suffer, while these
two disciples, instead of being compassionate and sym-
pathetic to their Teacher, were planning and desiring
other things. They misinterpreted Christ's words, and
thought He would go to Jerusalem and become a king,
whose glory would be greater than that of any other king.
So they put their mother up to asking Christ to give them
the highest offices in His Kingdom. They wanted to be
minister and prime minister. Don't be scandalized! The
Holy Spirit had not yet come to illumine them so they
could understand just what kind of kingdom Christ came
to establish in the world. Christ answered their request,
saying: "You do not know what you are asking for" (Matt.
20:22). And really, they did not know what they were
asking for, because a short time later, on Christ's left and
right hand would be two...robbers!

The same words Christ said to James and John may
also be said to those who ask for foolish or sinful things.
They don't know what they are asking for. Someone
bought a ticket and prayed to win the first prize. When
he learned that he had won, he went insane owing to
his excessive mirth and ended up in an asylum. Would
it not have been better for him to have remained poor
and kept his sanity, than to get rich and lose his mind?
What can a madman do with millions of dollars?

And those who fall into shameful love and insist on
being united with a certain person – do they know what
is in store for them? There are many examples of men
and women who turn the world upside down to get a
certain person as a companion, and once they succeed
in violating divine and human law to join with that person, they find sorrow and misfortune instead of joy

and happiness.... They do not know what they are asking for.

Someone has rightly said, that men blind with passion cannot see what is in their best interest. They are like the little child who sees hot coals glowing, and not knowing what would happen if he touched them, runs to grab them. But his mother who sees him, yells and takes him away from the fire.

Some may say: "I am not asking God for anything foolish or sinful, all I want is my health. I am the head of the family, and I ask for help because I have a lot of trouble. I have a daughter ready for marriage, and I ask for her good marriage. I want my son to find a job and to live well...."

No one can blame people for making such requests. But even in these cases, if we are Christians laboring and toiling for what is good and beautiful, we must leave our requests up to God's judgement. If God sees that our requests will truly be to our benefit, He may then give them to us; otherwise He will not.

O Heavenly Father! Not our will, but Thine be done.

THE REMAINING TIME

"That we may complete the remaining time of our lives in peace and repentance, let us ask of the Lord."

This, my beloved, is a new request. We ask it of God through the priest following the Great Entrance. Our homily will be based on this petition. We hope that you are following this series with interest. In simple words we are trying to present the grandeur of Orthodox worship.

Our Church invites us to pay attention to a precious thing in this petition, something more valuable than gold. This precious thing is time. Has time run out? Have we let the hours of the year pass spiritually unexploited? We are not able to regain them; we cannot turn back the wheel of time. Like lightning it flashes by, and woe to that person who is not willing to exploit the precious opportunities which are given for his spiritual progress, for his salvation.

Unfortunately, if there is one thing to which we do not pay attention, thereby losing it, it is time. The pleasures, enjoyments, and the various charms of this world hypnotize people, and thus they do not realize how the night passes away, how the day disappears. They waste time, they kill time, they live indifferently and apathetically. And the curious thing is that not only are just the young living this way, but also the elderly, those whose hair has turned white and are approaching the end. Even they do not realize how time has flown, that they must quickly do whatever is necessary for their salvation. They think that they will live here on the face of the earth eternally. The instinct of life is deeply rooted in human existence; man wants to live, not to die. Even when death approaches, stretching out his black wings, man stays glued to earthly things, hoping the thread of life will not sever, but he will conquer the crisis of illness; that he will live, reach into the very depths of old age, and become an eternally living being.

No one knows exactly how much time he will have here on earth, for God has concealed this secret from man. As the day and hour of the second coming of the Lord is unknown, in the same way the day of our death is unknown; it comes like a thief in an hour when we do not expect it. The day of our death is unknown.

How many years, dearly beloved, will we live here on earth? What remains of our time? Years? Months? Days? Hours? It's unknown. It is even possible for this to be the last day of our life, for this hour to be the final one.

It does not matter how much time remains. The important thing to be attentive to is that we do not let it slip away negligently and indifferently, but that we exploit it spiritually.

There are those who feel they are turning towards the sunset of their lives, and are anxious. But this is a worldly anxiety, full of earthly desires. They would like to live in order to finish this or that, and not to leave unfinished burdens for their families. They would like to be alive to see their daughter happily married and their son to finish his studies and receive his diploma. They want to live to finish certain worldly projects which they have started, but are only half-finished. And while it is true that people must be energetic and active and not lazily fritter away time, a way of life condemned by our Church, it is not right to spend it all on only these cares. There are other matters, purely spiritual, superior to all the others, which must be pondered seriously. Nor must the time taken up by these matters be considered wasted.

The Church points out two great themes for us in this petition. One is inner peace, the other is repentance. "Lord we entreat Thee, help us to pass the remaining time of our lives in peace and repentance."

Peace! Is there any blessing more important than this? It is a calm conscience. It is that secret voice heard in the depths of the heart, when a person believes in and loves God and his neighbor, when he takes care not to wrong his fellow man. He does not disgrace and defile his personal life by doing wrong, nor does he neglect to do good. How happy is that man whose conscience does not smite him for perpetrating wrong or for omitting good!

The happiness of man depends mainly on this witness of conscience. A small paradise is created in the heart of a person who is faithful and dedicated to God, and the word of our Christ is fulfilled in that "The kingdom of God is in ourselves" (Luke 17:21). Do you want an example? A shepherd who is doing no wrong, but is living like an innocent lamb, is happy. It does not matter that he lives in a hut and experiences various sorrows and difficulties. This shepherd feels a contentment which is not known to a millionaire, who, though powerful and famous, has committed injustices and crimes. This rich and influential one, though enjoying every single material good that this world has to offer, deep inside himself hears the voice of his conscience continuously censuring him, leaving him no quiet, and turning his life into a small hell, a prelude of damnation.

"My God, give us peace."

But if a person sins and loses his inner peace, can he regain it? Yes, he can. Glory be to God, to our all-kind and most merciful Father. Repentance is the means by which a sinful person is able to find the peace which he has lost.

Have you committed sins? Do not despair, my brother. Do not say that there is no hope of salvation. No! Run to your spiritual father, who acts in Christ's name, confess, and he will remit your sins. We must be in a state of repentance not only when we confess, but always; every day our soul must be in a condition of repentance. Because there is no day – what I am really saying is – there is not even an hour in which man does not sin. He may not be sinning with the body, but he is sinning in thought. And sinful thought is sin. No one is clean from this filth, from this uncleansed sin, even if he lives for only a day.

Therefore we must ask God to give us two valuable riches: peace of soul and repentance. A person without such peace, without repentance, is the most unfortunate man on earth. Thus our petition must be continuous: "'To complete the remaining time of our lives in peace and repentance, let us ask of the Lord.'"

THE END OF OUR LIVES

This new petition, dear friends, is very important. In earlier times, when people had faith in God, they believed that life does not end here, but continues beyond the grave. They believed that there is a Judgement and Retribution, Paradise and Hell. In those days, Christians, hearing the priest addressing this petition to God, were moved inside and made the Sign of the Cross.

But even today, there are pious souls, who, upon hearing this petition, are moved inside and pray. A wise and very pious university professor used to tell me that this petition, which speaks of the end of our lives moved him very much and he prayed to God to make the end of his life "Christian, without torment, blameless and with good account."

By this petition, the Church reminds us of death. As a certain teacher of our Church says, nothing is more certain than death, and nothing is more unknown that the hour of our death. It is beneficial for us to think about death. It is a medicine which, when taken regularly, contributes to keeping our souls sober. When we think of death, we avoid doing evil and are more eager to do good. That is why not only Christians, but pagans, too, used to meditate on death, and wanted others to remind them of it. Philip, King of Macedonia, ordered a soldier to appear before him every morning and say: "Philip, do not forget that you are mortal."

Our lives are full of *temptations.* Satan, desiring our destruction, never ceases to bother us and tempt us, but he tempts us worst of all at the end of our lives. He does not know exactly when we will die, but by certain external signs, like illness, he knows that our end is near, and he hovers like a raven, ready to rush in and grasp his prey, our souls. A good example of this was Job. Who was Job?

As Holy Scripture describes him, Job was a blameless man, just, true, and God-fearing. Even when calamities came upon him, one after another, he was tried and remained faithful and devoted to God. He was shown to be a rock of patience. This rock, however, was shaken and in danger of falling to its complete destruction. When? When Job fell sick with a serious illness, when his whole body was leprous, and, poor and destitute, he was thrown out of the city. When it seemed that his end was approaching, satan used his most powerful weapons to fight against him: his friends and his wife. His three friends, who visited him during this terrible ordeal, not only failed to comfort him, but actually offended him and brought him to such a state of mind that Job was shaken and cursed the day he was born. The second weapon of satan, and most powerful of all, was his wife. Despairing of the calamities which befell their home, and seeing her husband in a miserable state of poverty and misfortune, she said to him, that there was no other course than to commit suicide. But Job overcame this temptation, was cured of his sickness, and lived many more years. His end was without suffering, blameless and peaceful.

The end of Judas' life, however, was not painless, blameless and peaceful. He started out well. He followed

Christ, heard His teachings, saw His miracles; he enjoyed great honor and favor in being Christ's student, seeing the times of the Son of Man which the patriarchs and prophets of the Old Testament longed to see but were not able. But Judas, after so many blessings, was defeated by the temptation of greed. He was caught in the devil's net and could not escape. His end was painful, disturbed and troubled. It was full of shame and disgrace. He was defeated by despair, the worst of all temptations, and he committed suicide. . . .

So many others started their life in a Christian way, but because they were not careful of satan, they ended up committing terrible crimes, or went into error and heresy, and though they once shone like stars in heaven, they fell and the end of their lives was not Christian.

We must therefore be careful during our lives. The hour of death is the last hour of our earthly lives. The cup of death is bitter. "Alas! What agony the soul endures when from the body it is parting," chants our Church. The devil tries to take advantage of these last moments. Often, friends and relatives around our sick bed, instead of consoling and helping us with their words, create an oppressive atmosphere.

But if the Christian does not wait for the last hour of his life to prepare for his journey to heaven, but is ever ready, living a life of faith and virtue, then he will spend the last moments of his life with God's grace with faith in His infinite mercy. He overcomes the final temptations and comes out the victor. The end of his life is "without torment, blameless, peaceful." A little while ago, a pious old man in the city of Florina foresaw his end. He called his spiritual father, confessed, and received Holy Communion for the last time. He forgave all his enemies, gave his last counsels to his children and grand-children, and crossed his hands, surrendering his soul to the Lord. Truly, the end of this old man's life was "without torment, blameless, peaceful."

Another man lived his life far from Christ. He had every good thing. He had a wife and children, but no thought of God. One day came, however, when he changed completely. How? He saw a vision. He heard a voice, telling him that the end of his life had come, and he would have only seven more days to live. He believed in the vision and with the thought of having only seven days to live, he changed his way of life and spend all those days as God would want. The change was radical and his end was Christian. In peace he gave his soul to his Creator. If you would like to know more about this man, read the book, *Only Seven Days*. Only seven days! How much precious time we lose – the end of our life comes and we are still unprepared. . . .

"WITH WHOLE HEART"

Men of ancient times, as we said elsewhere, expressing feelings of worship to their gods, brought gifts to
them. These gifts were of many types. The most important were the sacrifices of animals. They offered sheep,
goats, and oxen.

When great calamities occured, droughts, floods,
plagues, wars, or revolutions, the pagans, believing that
their gods were angry because of their sins, thought they
could appease them if they offered sacrifices of people
instead of animals. They killed children and young
adults, and these horrible offerings were called human
sacrifices. The Christian shivers when reading the history
of these things.

Greece used to offer human sacrifice to their false
gods. There was a time when, in Macedonia, the river
Aliacmon was worshipped as a god. When the river
overflowed, they would offer children, and their blood
was blended with its waters. In this way they thought
the god could be appeased. And such things happened
everywhere – the situation was horrible.

But, thanks to God, Christ came to the world, and
by His teaching he abolished all these sacrifices which
could not erase the guilt men had because of their sins.
It is impossible for such blood to clean a guilty conscience. Only Christ, as God-man, voluntarily sacrificing Himself on Golgotha, succeeded where the countless

sacrifices of the ancients did not. One drop of the blood which fell from the pierced hands and feet of the Crucified One, only one drop, was enough to wash the sins of the world.

For whom? Not for all, but for those who believe in Christ, repent and decide to live according to His will. For them, Christ's sacrifice becomes deliverance and salvation.

This mystery cannot be explained by human language. It is understood by those blessed to believe in Christ.

Christ sacrificed Himself once, but His sacrifice continues to be offered on the Holy Altars of the Orthodox world when an Orthodox priest celebrates the Liturgy. It is offered bloodlessly. It is offered in the humble elements of bread and wine, which are mysteriously changed into the Body and Blood of Christ.

Three prayers accompany the offering of bread and wine, and these prepare the Mystery of *Holy Eucharist.* The first prayer is read at the end of the service of Prothesis, when the priest silently asks: "O God, our God, who didst send us the heavenly Bread, the Food of the whole world, our Lord and God Jesus Christ to ransom us, to do us good, to bless and sanctify us . . . ." The second prayer is said when the priest places the gifts on the Holy Table after the Great Entrance. The third, the most important of all, is said after the Exclamation, "Thy gifts of what is Thine . . . ." It begins with the words: "Again we offer unto Thee this reasonable and bloodless service and ask and pray and supplicate Thee: send down Thy Holy Spirit upon us and upon these Gifts here presented . . . ."

These three prayers, of equal importance, are connected with the Mystery of Divine Eucharist. We will talk more of the third when we come to that most important moment when the Gifts are consecrated. We will now speak about the second prayer, which is read while the Deacon says the petitions after the Great Entrance. It is as follows:

"O Lord God Almighty, Who alone art holy and dost receive the sacrifice of praise from those who call upon Thee with their whole heart, receive also the supplication of us sinners and accept it at Thy Holy Altar, and enable us to offer to Thee Gifts and spiritual sacrifices for our sins and for the ignorance of the people; look upon us as worthy to find grace in Thy sight, that our sacrifice may be well pleasing unto Thee, and that the Good Spirit of Thy grace may rest upon us and upon these Gifts offered here, and upon all Thy people."

This beautiful prayer tells us that all gifts and sacrifices that we, the faithful, offer are different from any other sacrifice the ancient world offered, because they are spiritual sacrifices. They are our prayers. They are our thanks for Christ's boundless love.

I would ask you to pay attention to one particular phrase in this prayer, "with whole heart." That is to say, we should love and pray to God whole-heartedly. This reminds us of the first of the Ten Commandments, where we are told to love God with all our spiritual and intellectual powers: "Thou shalt love the Lord thy God with all thy heart and with all thy soul and all thy strength" (Deut. 6:5).

Yes, we should *love God* with our whole heart. What does this mean? There are persons and things that we love. We love flowers, trees, birds, animals; we love people like our mother and father, wife and children. Love is the most noble emotion. Above all, however, we should love God, who created all the beauties of the earth. He created everything, He provides for all. He sent His Son for the salvation of the world. We should love Him with our whole heart, not half-heartedly. Alas! if we love persons and things more than God, the Lord of everything!

We should love God the way the saints, martyrs and confessors did. We should love him like St. Paul, who used to say that no person, thing or power could separate him from Christ's love (Rom. 8:35). All the water in the rivers or seas cannot extinguish divine love, which burns in the hearts of true Christians.

Unfortunately, however, this love has disappeared in this century of unbelief and corruption. We love everything except God.

You, though, dear Christians, who go to Church, and whom God allows to view the precious Gifts on the Holy Altar, you should pay attention at that time, so that your whole heart be directed to God. You should love God with your whole heart.

"LET US LOVE ONE ANOTHER"

After the chain of petitions read by the deacon, after the silent prayer of the priest, and after the exclamation, "Through the mercies of Thine only-begotten Son, with whom Thou art blessed, together with Thine all-holy, good and life-giving Spirit, now and ever and unto ages of ages," the priest turns to the people and says: "Peace unto all." That is to say, peace should reign in our hearts, no thoughts of hate or revenge — our inner world should be without turmoil.

And if the lay people's hearts should be calm, so too should be the heart of the priest. The celebrant should be present as a likeness of Christ. That is why the people, through the cantors, return the prayer of peace to the priest, saying: "And with thy spirit." This means, not only peace for us, but for you too. Woe to that priest who celebrates the Liturgy with hate or vengeance in his soul!

"Peace unto all." Unfortunately, these beautiful prayers for the peace of the clergy and laity do not reach people today. They are indifferent to them. The only thing they are thinking about is when the Divine Liturgy will be over, so they can leave the church and carry on their secular affairs.

"Peace unto all. And with thy spirit." With these words the Church desires to create a sacred atmosphere in the House of Worship, clear of all infection of hatred and enmity. We hear the deacon calling out in this sacred atmosphere: "Let us love one another, that we may with one mind confess." These words are a vibrant call to love. But what is this love the Church calls us to?

Love, dear friends, is a feeling that we do not have to learn from others. And because of its origin, this love is called *natural love*. It is taught by God. A mother, for example, experiences this love and does not have to be taught how to feel it by another person.

Without this natural love felt between mother and child, husband and wife, human society could not exist. This love is the link which unifies people. It is a secret affection felt by one human being for another, and as the stars are held in sway by universal attraction, not leaving their orbits, in the same way people are held in sway by another law, superior to the law of gravity — and this law is love, which God plants in our hearts.

But while the stars do not escape the universal law of gravity, we, being free creatures, can forsake the moral law of love. Thus, we see mothers killing their children before they are born or after they are born, women poisoning their husbands, husbands leaving their wives, children striking and killing their parents. . . , people acting like animals, or worse, because they uprooted the natural law of love from their hearts.

Love, under the influence of sin becomes distorted and corrupted. It is no longer natural and God-taught love. It became confined, as history shows, to closed circles of individuals. Ancient people, separated from their families, from their countries, loved no one else. The ancient Greeks, who boasted of their civilization, and were pagans, hated and turned away from other people, calling them barbarians, as if they were inferior beings. Even the Hebrews, who had a highly superior form of religion, had a very narrow idea of love.

But Christ, who came as Savior and Redeemer of humanity, took natural love, cleansed it of infectious, distortive and corruptive elements, and through His teachings and example, raised it up to the stars of heaven and gave it such depth and breadth, that Christ's love shone over the world like the sun. It gave light and warmed mankind, and as such, it appeared as a new commandment.

As Christ said, love became the most important mark of those who truly followed Him: "By this shall all men know that ye are my disciples, if ye have love one to another" (John 13:35). Christ told His disciples that people who live in the darkness of sin and error will understand that you are my disciples if you love each other. Love will distinguish you from all other people.

Truly, that which the ancient world lacked was not wisdom, rhetoric, arts or sciences, but spiritual love – a love which could stretch its wings to embrace all people – an infinite and universal love, wide like the sky and deep like the sea; a love which would have the Cross of Christ as its yardstick, for before this measure of love, every other means of measuring it are small indeed. Christ, raised on the Cross, calls His disciples, the faithful of all ages, to love as He Himself had loved.

The Apostles and Christians of the first centuries listened to Christ and followed His example. They showed this spiritual love, and the world with its wild hatred and vengeance saw it and marveled. Pagans, upon seeing the Christians' love, were converted and became Christians themselves, reasoning that the faith which possesses such a high teaching, and whose followers practice it in their everyday life, must be the true faith. The world never saw love like that of the early Christians.

If you would like to see how the Christians of the first centuries were, then open the Book of Acts and carefully read Chapter 4, verses 32-37.

Read also the First Epistle to the Corinthians, Chapter 13, where we find the *hymn of love*, where all the characteristics of Christian love are described, a love which did not remain a theory, but became practice.

Another who praised love was Christ's disciple, John the Evangelist. It is said of this Apostle, that when he became too old to preach to his Christians as he once did, he would go to the gatherings and, instead of preaching, would simply say: "Children, love one another." These words he would always say at the meetings, and when asked why he repeated these same words over and over, he answered that the one who loves keeps all the commandments of the Lord.

Therefore, "let us love one another, that we may with one mind confess."

"TRINITY, ONE IN ESSENCE AND UNDIVIDED"

Dear friends in Christ, let us continue our explanation of the Divine Liturgy.

In the ancient Church, when the priest or deacon said, "Let us love one another, that we may with one mind confess," the Christians in attendance kissed one another, and this pure and untainted kiss was an external expression of the love in their hearts. It was not simply a kiss of lips, but a kiss between souls, a spiritual kiss, which carnal contemporary people can neither believe in nor understand. Contemporary people understand and experience only amorous kisses. But the early Christians were so elevated and separated from material matters during the Liturgy, that it would not be an exaggeration to say that the kiss of those Christians was an angelic one. The church was a heaven; and people, angels.

But as the love between Christians began to grow cold, the sacred custom of kissing began to disappear and to be restricted only to the clergy. We are informed that, in the 13th century, instead of a kiss, it was customary to pass a small icon of the Crucifixion around to be kissed by everyone. Venerating the icon at this point, the Christians meant to say: "As Thou, O Christ, didst love the world, we, being imitators of Thy love, also walk and live in the world."

But even venerating such an icon has disappeared today.

The ancient kiss of love is restricted, as we said, to the celebrating clergy; but I would doubt that even this kiss among priests is a sincere expression of love. Unfortunately, in our times, even love among the clergy – bishops, priests and deacons – has diminished significantly, and in many cases, has disappeared. It is a rare thing for priests to love one another and kiss each other honestly. For this reason, Christians who are familiar with the kinds of disputes that take place among the clergy often speak sarcastically about the kiss between priests. Therefore, even the holiest things are in danger of becoming forms devoid of substance. O Lord, have mercy on us sinful and unworthy people, because we live in this century of hatred and corruption!

"Let us love one another, that we may with one mind confess . . . ," says the deacon. And the cantors, on behalf of the people, add: ". . . Father, Son and Holy Spirit; Trinity consubstantial and undivided," while the priest says: "I will love Thee, O Lord, my strength; the Lord is my Foundation, and my Refuge and my Deliverer" (Ps 17:1).

There are many people today, who praise and extol love, but do not want to learn about faith and dogma. They say: "Down with dogmas, these incomprehensible concepts, 'Love one another,' and that's enough . . . ." These people, however, do not think rightly, because "Love one another" (John 15:12), as well as every other moral teaching of Christianity, is based on the belief in one supernatural event, that Christ came from heaven to earth.

The injunction "Love one another" is not something solitary. It is connected with Christ's historical person – with the sacrifice that He offered on terrible Golgotha, where His love shone like the sun. Without this faith, love has no foundation. Without Christ's love, even natural love degenerates and is distorted, becoming a deceptive mask of human egotism.

God is the prototype of love in Christianity. But who is God? He is the God that Christ revealed to the world. Before Christ, the true God was unknown to the world. Everything was worshipped as a god except the true God. Only in one corner of the earth, the land of Israel, was there any knowledge of the true God, and this knowledge was not complete. The Israelites (Jews) were surrounded by idolaters and were in danger of falling into idolatry themselves. It was not possible to instruct them in the higher teachings about God. Whatever they learned from the God-inspired teaching of the Old Testament was certainly true, but it did not have the stature of the teachings that the Gospel has.

A certain teacher of the Church used to say: "If you wish to be taught who the true God is, go to the Jordan River, for there was revealed the mystery of the Holy Trinity. There was revealed the Father, the Son and the Holy Spirit, one God, one Deity, but distinguished in three Persons.

As the Great Athanasios taught, "so that we may venerate one God in Trinity and Trinity in Unity, neither confusing the Persons nor dividing the Essence." That is to say, the *Person* of the Father is one, the *Person* of Son another, and the *Person* of the Holy Spirit yet another, but the *Divinity* of the Father, the Son and the Holy Spirit is One. The glory of all three persons is equal, and their infinite eternity and majesty is the same. Whatever the Father is, so is the Son and the Holy Spirit. God is the Father, God is the Son, and God is the Holy Spirit, and in spite of this, they are not three Gods, but one.

The dogma of the Holy Trinity is the fundamental dogma of our Faith. It is the summit of all the truths of our Faith. Only by faith can someone perceive this. If a person does not believe in Christ, no matter how many arguments might bring forth, he lacks faith. Faith is a gift of God.

. The moral teachings are based on the dogma of the Holy Trinity, and one of these teachings speaks about unity among Christians. The Church emphasizes this unity with the: "Let us love one another, that we may with one mind confess. . . ." The meaning of this is that we are imperfect, we are sinners. We have hatred and hostility in our hearts. We are divided one from another. We hate and are hated. And even in the house of worship, the devil does not let us undisturbed. Sin has put us in such a state. But we can raise the eyes of faith to heaven and see the mystery of the Holy Trinity, and see the unity of the Three Persons of the Holy Trinity.

O Lord, Christ, we wish to be united with the Father and the Holy Spirit as Thou art, to have love for one another and be united, becoming a small likeness of the Holy Trinity. Thou art the model of this unity, Thou, O God, the God in Trinity.

Thus united, we will be able to attend the Divine Liturgy and chant: "Father, Son and Holy Spirit, Trinity one in essence and undivided."

"THE DOORS, THE DOORS. . ."

We are at the moment in the Divine Liturgy when the priests kiss each other, thus expressing the love they should have for one another, giving us the exhortation: "Let us love one another, that we may with one mind confess. . . ." After this, we hear: "The doors, the doors; in wisdom let us attend." What can this order mean, and why is it heard at this point in the Liturgy? It is these questions we will try to answer.

Our Lord Jesus Christ commanded His disciples: "Give not that which is holy unto the dogs, neither cast ye your pearls before swine, lest they trample them under their feet, and turn again and rend you" (Matt. 7:6). What do these words mean? Christ says, if you have pearls, precious stones, do not throw them to pigs. Pigs are not able to appreciate the value of precious things, and they will attack you. Pigs do not want diamonds, but want to live in mud. In the same way, no one gives valuable things to dogs. Christ was speaking in parables – dogs and pigs are those people who do not believe, and lead a bestial, unclean and sinful life. These people are in no position to appreciate the words of the Gospel and the holy mysteries which shine like diamonds. The holy dogmas and Mysteries of the Church should not be revealed to such people. They will scorn them.

The early Christians kept this admonition. They certainly tried to spread their Faith to others as much as possible. But if they met impudent people, who, like pigs and dogs, were ready to scorn and mock even the most sacred things, they did not reveal the grandeur of their Faith to them, but silently prayed to God to give them repentance, since "there is a time for everything." There is a time for Christians to speak, and a time not to. There is a time to reveal what is holy to believing people, and a time to hide and protect it from profane and impious people.

Because the precious gifts will be uncovered and blessed in only a short time hereafter, the Church with her exhortation, "The doors, the doors...," summons everyone's attention, especially that of those whose sacred duty it is to watch the doors of the church. In the early Church, there were Doorkeepers, people who watched so that unbelievers or those forbidden did not enter the church. Holy things are for believers, not for unbelievers. The doors of the house of worship in the ancient Church were closed as soon as the Liturgy of the Faithful began, and only the faithful who were going to receive Holy Communion remained in the church.

Today, however, there are no Doorkeepers, and the church doors remain open until the end of the Divine Liturgy, and so people of non-Christian religions and heretics, masons and atheists enter the church without any restriction, and remain there while the Liturgy is celebrated. In the Diocese of Florina, where I am responsible, I circulated an encyclical and ordered that all churches have Doorkeepers, and entrance forbidden to those dressed indecently.

"The doors, the doors..., let us attend!" Dear readers, in this century another kind of desecration of the holy is taking place. On Sunday, the Divine Liturgy is broadcast from radio stations. Can you imagine what is going on? At the most sacred moments, when the Liturgy is broadcast, impious people are joking and using obscene language, blaspheming and doing indecent things. Thus, the holy things which the Lord calls us to protect are being thrown to dogs and pigs, as Christ named the impious unbelievers.

What is taking place is a new desecration, and the responsibility of the Church is great, for if the Church took the words of Christ into consideration, she would not allow the entire Liturgy to be broadcast, but only up to the reading of the Holy Gospel, or even better, broadcast the Liturgy or some other special service with sacred readings and a short sermon only to the sick and those who could not go to Church.

"The doors, the doors, in wisdom let us attend." This order, historically justified in the practice of the ancient Church, can be interpreted also allegorically. Let me explain. According to St. Paul, every Christian attending church is himself a holy temple. The doors of this temple are the senses, especially sight and hearing. Through these, various impressions from the external world enter the soul. Therefore, in order not have our inner world infected by sinful sights and sounds, as well as by sinful thoughts, we need special attentiveness. As Holy Scripture says, "death is coming in through the doors" (Jer. 9:21), and as a teacher of the Church interprets this passage, a person's "doors" are his senses.

In one of his homilies, St. Basil the Great says: "Take care, for it is possible for a person to stand in the Divine Liturgy reverently and appear to be someone holy. And in spite of it, this person, if he does not care for his inner world, can be infected internally by thought and mentally commit sin. And it is terrible for someone to be in church in body, but mentally be somewhere else.

At this point, my dear brothers and sisters, I must sigh, for what clergyman or layman can boast that his mind is fixed on what is said and heard in the Divine Liturgy from beginning to end? Unfortunately, people become absent-minded so easily, so that they may be in church, and yet not there, and when they leave church, they can neither remember the Epistle, nor the Gospel, nor anything else whatsoever.

Therefore, beloved, when you hear: "The doors, the doors; in wisdom let us attend," let us force ourselves to be attentive and participate reverently in the entire Divine Liturgy, especially that part in which the miracle of miracles takes place, the consecration of the precious Gifts.

THE FIRST ECUMENICAL SYNOD

IV

THE SYMBOL OF
THE FAITH

THE GLORIOUS FLAG

In our previous homily, we explained the expression, "The doors, the doors; in wisdom let us attend." We spoke of the meaning this exhortation has. Heretics and unbelievers are not permitted to remain in church, and the faithful who remain should listen reverently and fix their thoughts on what is being said and done in the Liturgy. We said before and we repeat, that it is a sin when the celebrating priest recites the beautiful prayers and petitions, reads the Gospel and offers up the awesome Mystery, and the cantors chant: it is a sin to be there in body, but absent in spirit.

After "The doors, the doors...," complete silence should prevail in the house of worship. Everyone is waiting for something important to be said – and that which is heard immediately afterward is the Creed.

The Creed today is said by the reader. In the Russian and American Churches, the entire congregation says it. This is not an innovation, but an ancient tradition. It would be good if this ancient custom were revived throughout the entire Church. In our Diocese, we ordered the Creed and the Lord's Prayer to be said by the entire congregation. That way, the whole service of the Liturgy comes to life, and even the cold and indifferent person awakens when he hears the Creed being said aloud and feels that something worthy of attention is taking place.

And truly, the Creed is of great importance. It is called the sacred Symbol of our Faith. But what is a symbol? A symbol is something that gives us an immediate understanding of something accepted or believed. For example, the eagle in ancient times was a symbol, which, when seen depicted on a flag, was understood to mean that the state which had such a flag was the most powerful in the world, the Roman Empire. Another symbol was the double-headed eagle, depicted mainly on the flags of the Byzantine Empire. Today, the two superpowers, Russia and the United States, have respectively hammer and sickle, and 50 stars on their flags, while on the Greek flag is the symbol of the Cross.

As the various countries of the world are distinguished from one another by the special symbol representing them on their flags, our Church, the Orthodox Church, is distinguished from all other religions and heresies by Her Creed, heard during the Liturgy. The Creed is the sacred Symbol of the Orthodox Church. The Creed is our glorious "flag:" a flag under which all the faithful have fought and will continue to fight.

It is common practice that when the people recite the Creed, the priest in the Sanctuary, also reciting it, shakes the Aer above the Precious Gifts. The Aer is a rectangular piece of cloth, usually red in color, with which the Precious Gifts are covered until this point in the service. Therefore, since whatever is said or done during the Divine Liturgy has its own special meaning, let us briefly see what this act represents.

Certain interpreters of the Divine Liturgy say that the priest fans the Aer to keep insects out of the Chalice. One of the more recent commentators says that once a lizard fell into the holy Chalice from the ceiling of the

Sanctuary, and the pious priest ate the lizard because the body was soaked with the Blood of the God-Man. What faith and piety our priests had years ago! And what cold-heartedness and indifference exists today! The holy Chalice is considered an ordinary cup. . . .

But there is another interpretation: the priest fans the Aer over the Precious Gifts to show that our Creed is not a false one, like the others humanity follows, but the true Creed. It is, as we have said, our sacred symbol, the glorious flag of Christendom, which always defeats its enemies. And just as soldiers, when they conquer a high hill, raise their flag on the summit, letting it wave as if shivering with emotion, so our Church, which is like an army that fights and defeats unbelievers and heretics with the blood of the Sanctified Lamb, raises the Aer symbolically like a flag. This moment is like proclaiming Her victories and triumphs. It is like repeating the God-inspired saying of St. John the Evangelist: "This is the victory that overcometh the world, our faith" (I John 5:4).

The Creed has its history. It was composed by two Ecumenical Synods, the First and Second. The First convened in 325 A.D. at Nicea of Bithynia, Asia Minor, during the reign of Constantine the Great. Three hundred and eighteen fathers and teachers of the Church, martyrs and confessors who suffered when the persecutions were still going on, condemned the heresy of the Arians. The latter taught that there was a time when Christ, the Son of God, did not exist. Arius, their leader, denied the Divinity of Christ, as do contemporary Jehovah's Witnesses, the "spiritual" grandchildren of Arius.

The Second Ecumenical Synod took place in 381 A.D. at Constantinople during the reign of Theodosios the Great, with one hundred and fifty fathers and teachers in attendance. St. Gregory the Theologian acted as president of the Synod and condemned and excommunicated another heretic, Macedonios, who denied that the Holy Spirit was God.

The fathers and teachers of the First and Second Synods did not teach their own doctrines, but interpreted rightly the various passages of the Holy Scriptures which the heretics distorted and misinterpreted. The fathers formulated a short statement of the most fundamental of all dogmas (teachings); the Holy Trinity. It is to these fathers and teachers of the Church that we owe eternal gratitude. The heretics of every century blaspheme them, but the Orthodox Church glorifies them, and on the day of the commemoration chants the following hymn of praise:

"When the choir of holy Fathers assembled from the ends of the inhabited world, it formulated the doctrine that the Father and the Son and the Holy Spirit are of one essence and nature; and it transmitted clearly to the Church the mystery of Theology. Honoring them faithfully by praise, let us pronounce them blessed, saying: O divine army; O soldiers of the camp of the Lord, who speak of God; O most radiant stars of the spiritual firmament; O invincible towers of the mystical Sion; O fragrant flowers of Paradise; O all-golden mouths of the Logos; O boast of Nicaea, and ornament of the inhabited world, intercede fervently for our souls."

I BELIEVE...

In our last homily, we spoke generally about the Symbol of our Faith, the Creed, which is recited at every Divine Liturgy. The Creed is a short statement of the truths that every pious Christian should believe. Because it is short, even those with little formal education can learn and recite it by heart.

In the past, when faith was alive, not only educated people, but even shepherds and peasants listened to the Creed with great reverence, and considered it an honor to recite it in church. They enjoyed hearing or saying the Creed, that sweet melody of the Holy Spirit. Children took pride in learning and reciting it by heart. Christians attending the Divine Liturgy blessed the parents of those children, who like angels, recited the sacred Symbol in their clear, unaffected voices.

That was then — but what about now? A pious priest once told me that some time ago in his parish, a scandal occurred because a man wanted to become a godparent of a child who was about to be baptized. The priest asked the godfather to recite the Creed, but the man said that he did not know it. So the priest gave him the book so he could read it, but he refused to do this. He was ashamed to read the Creed, and audaciously told the priest he didn't want to read the Creed. See what we are reduced to! Unbelieving people want to become godparents in sacramental services....

In our diocese, we issued an encyclical ordering priests to advise parents not to accept as godparents people who do not believe, or have caused scandal. Only people who truly believe and live according to God's commandments are to be godparents for people who themselves believe and live the Creed and try to transmit it to the children they baptize. Priests and parents who accept non-church goers as godparents commit a big sin, because they make a mockery out of the Mysteries and allow pearls to be thrown to swine.

The Creed is a short statement of the Orthodox Faith, as we have said. It consists of 174 words in Greek, and each word has its own deep significance. An attempt to discuss the entire content of the Creed would result in many homilies. It would end up as another book. A brilliant preacher and author, Konstantinos Kallinikos, of blessed memory, wrote a very important book with the title, "The Foundations of the Faith," which in 31 lessons interprets and analyzes each article of the Creed. This book we recommend especially to teachers, professors, and scientists. They will find in it an excellent apology of the truths of our Faith. But here, we will endeavor to explain the content of the Creed in a few sermonettes.

The first words of the sacred Symbol are "I believe." Let's take a few everyday examples to help us understand what "belief" is, because belief (faith) is not only necessary for religious life, but even for daily worldly existence itself.

You are a stranger in a city. Noontime comes, and you are hungry. You enter one of the many restaurants and are given a meal, cooked by a cook you do not know. You eat it with pleasure, but also with faith, that is, with confidence, because you yourself didn't see the materials with which the cook prepared the meal, and you didn't watch its preparation from beginning to end. You eat the food, however, having faith – confidence – in the restaurant owner. If you did not have faith in him, then you would never have sat down to eat in his restaurant.

You walk somewhere by yourself. You want to go to a place some distance away, but you don't know the way. You meet a stranger and ask him, and in a kindly manner he shows you the way. You have faith, confidence in what the stranger tells you, and you go as he directed you.

Now, you want to travel by car, train, or airplane. You don't know who the drivers or pilots are. Yet in spite of that, you enter the vehicle without investigating their capabilities, believing in them.

Another example. You fall sick and call the physician. He gives you a prescription to buy some medicines. And you, having faith in the doctor, follow his instructions; again, having faith in the pharmacist, you buy his medicines.

These examples, and many more, show that even in worldly matters, nothing can be done without faith. If faith were removed, all human activity would cease. Even the sciences would come to a halt: based on experiment, they will not be able to make any progress, since they begin their research on certain principles not yet proven, and they build the rest of their scientific investigations on these.

We live by faith. We believe in bakers and cooks. We believe in drivers of trains and airplanes. We believe in teachers and professors. We believe in scientists, diplomats and politicians. We believe in everything and everybody, only we do not want to believe in God.

Credulous to all, faithless and unbelieving in God.

O Disbelief! A philosopher of the ancient world, discussing the strangeness of human behavior, said that we believe in those people and things we should not believe in, and disbelieve the people and things we should believe in, thereby bringing great calamity to the world. How right he was! It would be enough to show the horrible state to which entire nations fell when they put their trust in persons and things that, in the end, deceived them and led them into great catastrophes.

The faith of the Christian, however, is not like faith of worldly men, who put their trust in people and worship idols and fantasies. The Christian knows in whom he believes. And out of the mire of unbelief, he cries aloud his belief: "I believe in one God, the Father almighty, Maker of heaven and earth, and of everything visible and invisible...."

THERE IS A GOD!

"I believe in one God..."

Dear readers, there are many subjects which people busily discuss, wherever they live and whatever their education, but the one topic above all others is that pertaining to God's existence. People are never indifferent to this subject. Even though some may appear indifferent, there come moments in their lives when this matter sets them off. Is there a God, yes or no? If there is not, then everything is permissible, even the most heinous crimes. If He exists, however, then things are different, and everyone is responsible to the Creator for his actions.

God's existence is bound together with the notion of divine justice, a justice that is free of the imperfections and weaknesses of human justice and is able to punish every crime and reward every virtue. This is what St. Paul means when he says: "But without faith it is impossible to please Him; for He that cometh to God must believe that he is, and that He is a rewarder of them that diligently seek Him" (Hb. 11:6).

Faith in the existence of God constitutes the cornerstone of the Christian edifice. That is why the first thing proclaimed in the symbol of the Faith is the existence of God: "I believe in one God."

Unbelievers have multiplied in our century and fight brazenly against God, saying and writing in books and magazines that there is no God. If you ask an unbeliever, however, what his arguments are against God's existence, you will see that he does not have a serious argument. He accuses the Church of dogmatism, that She tells us to believe without proof, but he himself presents as a dogma that there is no God, and the world must accept that!

While atheism, old or new, feels it does not have to present any proof of what it maintains, it feels that the Church, which preaches FAITH in God's existence, must present *many* evidences with which to convince any impartial person.

God exists. Countless voices cry this. Let me give a few simple examples:

We are familiar with the camera. You stand before this machine and it takes your picture. If someone tells you the camera you are holding was not made in a factory, but created itself, would you believe him? Certainly not! And if your friends insists, you would begin to doubt his sanity, for only a person devoid of reason would say that cameras create themselves....

But there is a camera infinitely superior to any camera in the world. It will function for years, without expense; it takes millions of photos. What kind of camera is this? It is our eye. This is a perfect camera, a miracle. Who made it? If someone cannot accept that an ordinary camera is a work of chance, then how will he dare to say the eye is a work of chance? No, the eyes are not products of chance. Someone made them, and that someone is God. An eye is enough to demonstrate God's existence.

Do you know about radar? It is a huge artificial ear, which science took great pains to plan and produce. It is placed high on mountains and receives the sounds that airplanes or other objects produce, no matter how high they fly. Let someone dare insist that radar invented itself. No one would believe him. Everyone accepts that radar apparatus is designed by men and made in factories.

Do you admire radar? Then you must admire incomparable more human radar – the ears. Its construction and function astonishes scientists called otorynolaryngologists. Radar is created by man, the ears by whom? Certainly by someone, and that someone is God. An ear is enough to prove that God exists.

Yet another example. A city is supplied with water by an aqueduct, which has its reservoir outside the city. From there, the water flows through large and small pipes and reaches all the houses in the city. Aqueducts are admirable, as is the Athenian aqueduct, having an enormous reservoir. The network of pipes supplying the entire city has a total length of many thousands of miles. I ask you, who would dare say that such a huge system is a work of chance? No one with a sound mind would!

But let us look at another aqueduct which works day and night to supply not water, but blood to the human organism. The heart collects blood like a small reservoir, but does not hold it. It distributes it with absolute justice. Instead of pipes, it uses veins and arteries, which reach even the smallest parts of the body. There are capillaries thinner than a hair: imagine a tiny pipe like a hair and through it blood is flowing, reaching the tiniest parts of the anatomy. Do you admire the aqueduct? How much more should you admire the heart, which with an astonishing network of veins and arteries continuously distributes blood. If the heart stops working, the man dies in a few minutes. Engineers and technicians construct aqueducts, but who constructed the heart? Certainly someone, and this someone is God. A heart suffices — what am I saying — a hair-like capillary suffices to show that God exists!

We could present yet more examples; but there are so many, they would fill a whole book.

God exists! Reason demands it. God exists! The universe proves it from the grandest to the humblest creations. God exists! History testifies to it. God exists! Man's conscience proves it.

Our faith is not without proofs and arguments. Let everyone then, from the bottom of his heart declare his belief: "I believe in one God...!"

WHAT IS GOD?

*"I believe in one God, the Father almighty, Maker of heaven
and earth and of everything visible and invisible."*

God exists, dear friends, God exists! It is declared in
the first article of our Symbol. Millions of voices proclaim it. Atheism, as we said, has no evidence; it merely dogmatizes. And, as we have noted with atheists and
unbelievers, there come certain moments even in their
lives when they question their attitudes regarding this
most relevant subject. There are also examples old and
new concerning people, who, in quiet and peaceful times
made much noise, saying 'there is no God,' but when
the blue skies of their life became clouded, when trials
and tribulations shocked them and all their worldly foundations were shaken, when they faced catastrophe, then
those unbelieving atheists were humbled and they knelt
down to pray.

God exists, but what is He? This is another question.
Human reason, proud, restless, and searching, directs
itself also to the investigation of this topic. What can we
say? We can answer only briefly:

We have said that the question of the existence of
God is the highest and most important of all problems.
Every other subject is inferior to this lofty question. I
ask you, has *anything* been investigated to complete
resolution? Have answers been given to questions concerning, not only spiritual matters, but material things,

things that we can perceive with our bodily senses? Has science given answers even to questions like: "What is matter?" "What is light, electricity, magnetism, atomic energy?"

As we said some time before, science investigates various material phenomena, but it cannot explain them, it cannot give the final word concerning our existence, the creation, the energies and their sundry manifestations. These matters are shrouded in mystery. A philosopher once said, that in spite of all science has discovered, we are yet ignorant of many things and will continue to be so, because everything we know is a very small part of what we do not yet know.

We are ignorant, then, to a great degree concerning material things which we can perceive; how then we pretend to know those things that we cannot perceive, things that are above the material and constitute the spiritual world?

Human reason is not limitless, as some philosophers say; it has certain boundaries it cannot cross. Beyond the natural world is another world, the spiritual, supernatural world. We cannot perceive this world with our bodily senses, but we can do so with our spiritual senses – our faith, appropriately called "the sixth sense."

Our minds are limited. Let me cite an example:

Let us assume that an ant is crawling on a column of the Acropolis. The ant has a mind, that is, it reacts instinctively. We ask you, is it possible for the ant to comprehend and explain the architectural wonder? Certainly not. It's thought processes are far too limited. Humanity, like the ant, lives and walks, and even flies in space, seeing before it the expanse of the vast divinely-created kingdom. But human thought, no matter how developed, cannot comprehend or explain divine creation in all its magnitude and profundity. Man stands on a pinhead of the immense universe. As an ant cannot comprehend the architectural plan of the Acropolis, so the little human being, with his limited reason, is incapable of understanding the details of the Divine Creator's plans. That is why the Apostle Paul, astounded by the mysteries of divine wisdom, says: "O the depth and riches of the wisdom and knowledge of God! How unsearchable are His judgements and His ways beyond understanding! For who hath known the mind of the Lord? Or who hath been His counsellor?" (Romans 11:33-34).

And in spite of this, humanity in its pride insists on investigating the Incomprehensible. A lyric poet, Simonides, was once invited to the palace of an ancient king and was asked to answer a question: What is God? The poet asked him to give him a day to think about it. When the day had passed, the poet appeared before the king and asked him to give him another two days to think it over. It was granted. When the two days had passed, the poet requested that time to be doubled, four days. The king grew impatient because of the delay, and when the poet asked twice the previous amount of time, the king asked why. The poet answered, "The more I investigate the matter, the more difficult it appears to be."

What is God? A definition would be beyond the capabilities of the human mind.

One of the greatest fathers and teachers of the Church, St. Augustine, in discussing this topic, begins a moving dialogue with Creation. Let us listen:

"I asked the earth, 'What is God?', and she answered: 'I am not your God.' Everything in Creation that I asked gave me the same answer. I asked the sea and the depths and all that live and swim in the seas and oceans, and all in common answered: 'I am not your God; search for Him higher.' I asked the winds that blow and the air, and the creatures that live in it, and they answered me: 'I am not your God.' I asked the sun, the moon and the stars. 'We are not the God you seek.' Then I said to all that surrounded me: 'You say you are not my God. Tell me then what do you know about Him?' And all answered in a loud voice, 'God made us. God is our Maker, our Creator!'"

In spite of all the wisdom our ancient forefathers had, the true God remained unknown to them, and for this reason, an altar was erected in Athens, the capital of arts and sciences, with the inscription: "TO THE UNKNOWN GOD" (Acts 17:23). The unknown God was revealed to the world through the revelation of Jesus Christ, our Lord. And the God that Jesus Christ revealed is the true God. He is *spirit*. He is *light*. He is *love*. We worship and adore Him, and this faith we proclaim by saying: "I believe in one God, the Father almighty, Maker of heaven and earth and of everything visible and invisible."

DO YOU BELIEVE?

"And in one Lord, Jesus Christ, the Son of God...."

The first article of the Symbol, the Creed, speaks about God. Continuing now, we will discuss the second article. It reads, "And in one Lord, Jesus Christ, the only-begotten Son of God, begotten of the Father before all ages. Light of Light, True God of True God, begotten, not made, consubstantial with the Father, through Whom all things were made."

The first word of this article is "and." This "and" was not introduced unintentionally into the Symbol – none of the words of the Symbol are there by accident. Every word has significance. After much contemplation and by the illumination of the Holy Spirit, the fathers of the First and Second Ecumenical Synods composed the Symbol and placed each word properly. The word "and," then has its own significance. It connects the second article with the first. It places the Father and the Son on the same level, the same plane. God is the Father, and God is the Son, the Christ, as well. The "and" means that we believe in God the Father, and we believe in His Son, our Lord Jesus Christ.

Those fathers with all the martyrs and confessors believed in Christ. They believed what the Symbol of the Faith proclaims about Him. Twentieth-century people, however, even those who call themselves Christians, do they really believe in Christ?

If you ask people today, you will see that very few actually believe in Christ and strive to live in accordance with His holy will. The rest? If they went to universities and consider themselves scholars or scientists, some then say Christ was a wise man, the wisest of all; others say He was a friend of the poor; others, that He was a great orator and sociologist; others, that He was a great revolutionary figure, who came to overthrow the establishment. None of them, however, in spite of the laudations they give Him, accepts what the Church believes. They do not accept Him as God. Others in our times go even further, into unbelief and atheism, and as they maintain that there is no God, they say and write that Christ never existed, except in people's imagination.

What a horrible thing unbelief is! If one begins to question his faith, without noticing it, he will begin to fall into greater and greater doubt, until he ends up an unbeliever. Such a person is like a rock – once it begins rolling down a hill, it will not stop rolling, but will continue until it reaches the lowest place it can find.

The faithless cry: "There is no God." But no matter how much they cry out, they will never succeed in blowing out the Faith of Christ. This faith has very deep roots in the human heart, and no satanic power is able to uproot it. The "I believe in one Lord, Jesus Christ, the only-begotten Son of God" will continue being declared boldly by every pure and humble soul. An old man once came from a neighboring village to the city of Florina and entered the diocesan office. He brought a little girl with him, who was attending the second grade of the elementary school. She was his granddaughter, and he had brought her to the office because she wanted to say the Creed before the Bishop. And so, she recited it in a lucid voice, and without error. I asked her if she believed in Christ, and she answered, correctly making the sign of the Cross, saying: "I believe in Christ and I love Him." I rejoiced and glorified God, because there are still pure, child-like souls.

Unbelievers continue to cry out and say that Christ never existed. But, that Christ existed, that He was born in Bethlehem in the reign of Ceasar Augustus, that he lived and worked in Palestine, that he was crucified by Pontius Pilate, these events are actual and not imagined. Christ was a historical person. Historians of the First century attest to this: Josephus, Tacitus, Suetonius, and Pliny. Although the means of communication were primitive, although He came from a despised country, His fame as an extraordinary teacher, prophet and wonderworker spread far beyond the borders of His native Israel and reached Rome.

Foreign authors speak of Christ's existence, His life and deeds. These had no relations with Him, but they observed the events with an indifferent heart. It is certain that Christ was born and lived in Palestine. It is as certain as the fact that Alexander the Great was born in Macedonia, lived and was active there. We believe the few historians who bore witness to the historical existence of Alexander, and no one questions his existence. People, therefore, should not question the historical existence of the Christ. They should have more faith in the testimonies that credible people wrote about Christ with truthfulness and self-denial – the four Evangelists.

The four Evangelists testify to Christ. Although there are some small discrepencies among the four in some points, these discrepencies show that the four Evangelists worked separately, without consulting one another.

These four witnesses are alike in describing the same event; although one might pay attention to some detail which the others overlook.

Christ's existence is witnessed to by foreign writers, and mainly by the four Evangelists, the Apostle Paul, and the other Apostles. It is witnessed to by countless martyrs and confessors, who shed their blood for the Faith of Christ. It is witnessed to by God, the Heavenly Father, through a myriad of miracles that have taken place in the past and will continue to occur forever in His holy Name.

Dear friends, let us erase from our hearts every question which satan puts there regarding Christ's existence and life. By studying the holy Gospels, our hearts will be filled with admiration for the unique Icon of Christ. The questions and doubts will then be changed into exclamations of faith, and together, with child-like voices, we will say: "I believe in one Lord, Jesus Christ, the only-begotten Son of God, begotten of God before all ages....

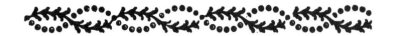

THE NAMES

"And in one Lord, Jesus Christ, the Son of God"

*C*hristian friends, there are twelve articles in the Symbol of the Faith. One of them, the first, concerns God. The following six concern Christ. The Creed consists of 174 Greek words. Most of them, 100, speak about Christ. Why is this? Because Christ was disputed by many unbelievers and heretics.

As we said in our previous homily, unbelievers questioned even Christ's historical existence, and heretics questioned and interpreted His life and acts in different ways, introducing theories which do not agree with Gospel teaching, and for this reason they were condemned by Ecumenical Synods.

From the day of Her conception, the Church held faith in Christ to be of great importance. Christ is the center, the Alpha and Omega, the beginning and end. When a man asked the Apostles "What must I do to be saved?", they answered: "Believe in the Lord Jesus Christ" (Acts 16:31).

But, who is Christ? The Symbol of the Faith answers this question. My brief answer is rather comprehensive, with words having deep meaning and requiring some explanation and discussion. Let us explain the first words of the second article: "And in one Lord, Jesus Christ, the Son of God."

As you see, Christ has four names. The first name is LORD. The second is JESUS, the third, CHRIST and the fourth, SON OF GOD.

These names are not simply words which have no relation to reality, like words without substance. They are names that correspond to reality. For example, someone has the name Anargyros. To have content and correspond to reality, the man bearing this name should be free from the love of money, in the manner of the holy Unmercenaries (Anargyroi). If he is miserly and greedy, however, then he bears this name in vain. The names that the Holy Scriptures give to Christ, however, do correspond to reality.

First, let us see what the name LORD means. Every man today is called by the title MISTER, which in most languages is the same word as LORD, and it's considered rude not to call him MISTER. But the lordship of man called MISTER, no matter how rich and powerful he is, is temporary and very limited, even if he holds command over many things. Today, rich, tomorrow poor. Famous today, tomorrow unknown and despised. Even if one owns many things and commands many people, this is not important. What is important is commanding one's own self, to rule and subjugate one's passions. If he lets his passions rule him, even though he is called LORD and SIR, he will in fact be a slave — a slave of passions and sin, a slave of satan. O man! you are but called LORD, but you have yet to truly become a LORD.

Man's lordship is limited. Little, trivial is this lordship compared to God's. God's power and dominion is limitless, and no one can find words to describe it sufficiently. In the Old Testament, the Hebrews did not dare pronounce God's name, but they used to say it by another, symbolic word, Yahweh or Jehovah. And as appears in many passages, Yahweh or Jehovah was seen, and appeared to many people, and He was Christ. St. Nectarios, Bishop of Pentapolis, wrote a book about this, and recently, Nikolaos Soteropoulos, a theologian, wrote a very important book with the title, "Jesus-Yahweh" (Athens, 1975). Christ as proved in a number of passages from the Old and New Testaments, is the Hebrew Yahweh and the Greek Kyrios (Lord) — they are one and the same.

Christ is Lord in an absolute sense. His domain is all creation, and consists of angels and men. Everyone is a subject of His domain, and even though some are wayward and do not obey Him, a time will come when even they will kneel before the Christ.

Christ is Lord. Open the Holy Scriptures and read the seventh chapter of the prophet Samuel. There you will see that the prophet Samuel saw a vision. He saw all the powers falling down in worship before the son of man, the Christ. The power, which appeared as an external power, had no end. St. John the Evangelist in the last book of the New Testament, Revelation, also saw Christ in a vision. He saw Christ seated on a white horse and crowned with many crowns, holding a sword. He was dressed in bright red and was called "King of Kings and Lord of Lords" (Rev. 19:16).

Christ is Lord with a capital L. His other name is Jesus. This is a Hebrew name which means savior. Many people who offered the world a great service have been named saviors, but the salvation they offered is insignificant in comparison to the salvation that Christ offers. The angel said to the Virgin Mary that the child born of her would save people from sin.

And the stories of millions of people who repented and were saved justifies the name given to the Child of Bethlehem at the angel's command. A lesser image of Jesus the Savior is a great man of the Old Testament, Joshua (Jesus son of Nun), a shadow of the great Savior.

The second Person of the Holy Trinity is also called by the name CHRIST. Those who believe in His Gospel have been called Christians, after this dear name. Why is Jesus called this? Because those Old Testament men who were destined to become kings of Israel were "christened" so with holy oil. Jesus was "christened" the king of the New Israel. He was ordained in the Jordan river as a man by the Holy Spirit and is now reigning over and governing His spiritual kingdom, the Church.

Christ is the Messiah whom people were awaiting. He is the Teacher. He is the High Priest and King of the Universe. To Him belongs all honor and glory, forever.

Say, then, my Christian friend: "I believe...in one Lord Jesus Christ, the only-begotten Son of God."

THE SON OF GOD

In our last homily, we saw what the names, LORD, JESUS, and CHRIST mean. In addition to these three names, the second article of the Symbol of Faith adds yet another name when it speaks about Christ. The name is SON OF GOD.

Christ is the Son of God. About this we will now speak. The subject is very difficult, but very necessary for our salvation. Let us invoke the Holy Spirit to enlighten us to sense and understand the truth contained in these few words.

Once, when Christ was alone with His disciples in a desolate place, He asked them a question: "Who do men say that I, the Son of man, am?" (Matt 16:13). That is to say, when people hear my teaching and see my miracles, what is their opinion of me? The disciples answered: Some say you are John the Baptist; others, that you are Elijah the Prophet; others, that you are Jeremiah; and still others, that you are one of the prophets of the Old Testament returned from the dead.

As we can see from the disciples' answers expressing the impression Christ gave to those who saw Him, everybody except His bitter enemies admired Him and considered Him an excellent person, a great personality, who, by what He said and did, was able to emulate historic persons of the Old Testament. But they thought no further. And this is still happening today. People of our times, like the ancient Jews, admire Christ as a great man in world history, but they stop there.

After this answer, Christ asked a second question: "Who do you say that I am." (Matt 16:16). That is, people who hear me have this notion about me, thinking I am one of the prophets; but you, who live with me, what do you think about me?

Peter, who was the most ardent of the disciples, answered the question: "Thou art Christ, *the Son of the living God."* Upon hearing Peter's confession, Christ said: "Blessed art thou, Simon Bar-jona: for flesh and blood hath not revealed it unto thee, but my Father which is in heaven." He enlightened your mind and you said it. This is a truth. And on this truth, like on a firm, unshakable rock, I will build a Church, and no power of satan will ever be able to destroy it.

What Peter confessed in that desolate place the Church is still preaching and will continue to preach until the end of time.

O my Christ! You are the Son of God, living and reigning forever.

When Christ was arrested and brought before the Jewish Court and the High Priest asked Him, "Art thou the Son of the Living God?" if Christ had answered "no" to this question, the accusations would have been dissolved and Christ would not have been condemned to death; but Christ answered with a firm and unshakable "yes," because His answer, "Thou hast said," means "Yes." The High Priest understood it to mean "yes," and that is why, when he heard, he was horrified, tore his clothes, and said that Christ had blasphemed because He made himself out to be the Son of God, adding, "We do not have further need of witnesses" (Matt 22:63-65).

Now the question is put to us: What did Christ mean when He said He was the Son of the living God, for even we are called sons of God and raise our eyes to heaven and call God "Father." We are children of God, but Christ's name of Son of God differs greatly from our being called sons of God. Christ is not the Son of God by calling, but by nature. He is of the same essence, consubstantial. He is not a creation, like us. We are of a different essence, a different substance.

Are the things we discuss too difficult? Let's try to simplify them:

Our existence in this world is limited. There was a time when we did not exist. We were born and came into the world at a certain point in time. We live in the world for a few years until the time comes to die, and we end our bodily life. Our soul does not die, it's immortal; however, we are speaking about bodily existence. While we live but a short time, Christ, as Son of the living God, was born in a way beyond our understanding, *before all ages,* before Abraham and Noah, before Adam, before the creation of the angels and archangels. There was not a moment in all of time when Christ did not exist, and to use theological language, we say, "As the Father exists, so exists the Son and the Holy Spirit: O Holy Trinity, glory to Thee!"

It is in this sense, which we in some way explained, that the Holy Scriptures refer to Christ as the Son of God, and this is declared as a truth of the Faith in the Symbol of the Faith.

Unfortunately, a man named Arius did not accept this fundamental truth of our Church. He admired Christ as a man, preached His grandeur, confessed His miracles but did not accept Him as God. He maintained that Christ is the first creation, superior to the angels and archangels, but lower than God. He preached that there was a time when Christ did not exist. This is the horrible heresy of Arius, and it is this heresy the Jehovah's Witnesses teach today, and they blaspheme St. Athanasios the Great while honoring the arch-heretic Arius.

The heresy that Christ is not True God, but a creation of God, was condemned by the First Ecumenical Synod. The Synod declared Christ to be consubstantial with (of the same essence as) the Father. The followers of Arius fiercely fought against this "consubstantial." At one point they wanted to add one letter to the Greek word for consubstantial, "homo-ousios," "i," iota, in order to call Christ homoi-ousios (of a similar essence) instead of homo-ousios (of the same essence).

The Church did not want to add this iota and struggled greatly, and the Symbol of the Faith remained unchanged. Together with the Saints and Confessors, let every one of us proclaim: "I believe in one Lord Jesus Christ, the only-begotten Son of God, begotten of the Father before all Ages. Light of Light, True God of True God, begotten, not made, consubstantial with the Father, through Whom all things were made."

THE SON OF MAN

*"Who for us men and for our salvation came down
from Heaven, and was incarnated by the Holy Spirit
and of the Virgin Mary . . ."*

Our Lord is a sign that has been contradicted. People have made war over His name. This began on the day of His birth and continues to this day, and will go on until the end of the world. No other person in history was fought over so much as Christ. Unbelievers and atheists reject Him; heretics teach ideas which are contrary to the Holy Scriptures and our Sacred Tradition. Heretics, egotists that they are, interpret the Holy Scriptures as they wish and think they have discovered something new. Some of them dispute the *divinity* of Christ, others question the humanity of Christ. Who are they?

They are the heretics who, on one hand accept that Christ is God, but on the other, do not admit that Christ became a man like us. They reject Christ's human nature. They maintain that the body with which Christ appeared on earth was not real, but an imaginary one. They think they are elevating Christ in this way, saying He did not have any real relationship with human flesh. They consider it degrading to say that Christ took on human flesh and became a real human being.

The heretics who rejected Christ's divinity were the Arians, the ones who rejected Christ's humanity were called Docetists. The Church, however, fought both

Docetism and Arianism. St. John the Evangelist says, concerning those who reject the truth that Christ took on human flesh, that they have the spirit of the Antichrist (II John 7).

Christ, who called Himself the Son of God, also referred to Himself as the Son of Man. Eighty times in the New Testament, Christ is called the Son of Man; and He is called so to emphasize that, besides having a Divine Nature, Christ also has Human Nature, which came with His birth from the Virgin Mary. He was made flesh and dwelt among us (John 1:14).

Christ is perfect God, but perfect Man as well. The Gospels, which describe the details of His earthly life, show that He was a true man, similar to us, and not a ghost or a phantom like those seen in dreams. As we can see in the sacred texts, Christ became hungry and thirsty, felt pain, cried and felt the need of rest and sleep – He slept on the deck of a ship and under the shade of trees; His immaculate hands and feet were pierced by nails, His side by a soldier's lance, and blood and water came out (John 19:34).

These things were written by eye-witnesses, the Evangelists. They are not fantasies, but real events. Over and over again, Christ, speaking about the time of His suffering, refers to Himself as "Son of Man." When asked where He lived, that he might be visited, Christ answered that even the wild beasts have their nests, but "the Son of man hath not where to lay His head" (Matt 8:20). Christ lived like the very poor, and tasted the sorrows and sufferings of human nature. He did not live outside the world, but in the midst of it with its suffering people, felt their pains and sorrows, and "the Son of Man" cried with them.

Christ is perfect man and perfect God. This is the teaching of our Church, a teaching which is not arbitrary, but based on the Holy Scriptures. And whoever questions the divinity or humanity of Christ is outside both the letter and spirit of the word of God.

But unbelieving heretics, upon hearing this teaching about the Christ, are scandalized and ask: "How is it possible to unite the divine and human natures?" We reply that the union of divine and human nature in the Person of Christ is truly a great mystery. As the Apostle Paul says, "And without controversy great is the mystery of godliness: God was manifested in the flesh, justified in the Spirit, seen of angels, preached unto the Gentiles, believed on in the world, received up into glory" (I Tim. 3:16).

An example will give us some faint image of this mystery. We say that the two natures were united in Christ "unconfused, unaltered, unchanged, and indivisible", but let us briefly look into every man and we will see the union of two dissimilar things. One is the body, the other is the soul. The first is perishible, the second imperishible; one visible, the other invisible; one natural, the other supernatural; one is material, the other immaterial. In spite of this, however, these are united in man. How? It is a mystery! Therefore, as these are united in man, in a similar manner the two natures, divine and human were united in Christ.

Yes Christ is a perfect man. But how? Wasn't there a *perfect man* before Christ? Our answer: the first man, Adam, was created without sin. He was created with wonderful psychic powers, which, when used rightly, would have given him continuous progress towards perfection and he would have become like God. But as we all know, the first man, Adam, did not remain in the state in which God placed him. He sinned. He made bad use of his divine gifts, and instead of being elevated, he fell. All men, who came from Adam, became corrupt, and their wickedness and bad habits, their crimes, impiety and unbelief began to conceal that beautiful image in man. They cried and moaned for their corruption and felt the need of someone from heaven to restore the image, to save mankind.

The one for whom men and nations were waiting appeared. He is Christ. He is the New Man, the New Adam, the Son of Man. Christ, with His virtues, appeared in the world, becoming the image – and not just an image, but *the* original image, namely the unique, excellent example of virtue, for people to look to and imitate.

With Christ as a prototype, people again become truly human, with all the depth and breadth the word contains, while outside of Christ, man is dehumanized, losing every element of nobility, exhibiting not the image of Christ, but that of Antichrist.

THE ALL-HOLY VIRGIN

*"And was incarnated by the Holy Spirit and of
the Virgin Mary, and became man."*

Dear friends, humanity is the summit of earthly
creation, and if God created nothing else, mankind
would be enough to testify that there is a God, an all-
wise God, omnipotent and benevolent. What an excellent creation man is! We see a beautiful statue and
admire it, and no one dares to say the statue created itself
without the sculptor. But, when compared to a human
being, what is a statue, even the most perfect one kept
in a museum and considered a treasure of infinite value?
The statue is dead, inanimate, idle. It has eyes but does
not see, ears but does not hear, feet, but cannot walk.
Man, however, is alive, with soul, an active and creative
statue, which when studied more and more gains more
and more admiration. Common sense says that, just as
every statue was made by an artist, man was created
by God.

Man is a marvellous creation of God, a little bit less
that the angels, and is divided into man and woman. Man
and woman are equal. They have the basic characteristics of human personality, reason, conscience, will and
the rest. They do possess differences, but the differences
between man and woman does not reduce, but rather
enhance the admiration due to humanity. They add
beauty and charm, making human life a pleasant thing.

Since the first man until now, billions of people have been born. Of these billions of people, men and women, there have been some who have tried to destroy the grandeur of humanity by their criminal acts, they tried to degrade the human personality and put the human race to shame. Mankind fell from that lofty height of honor and dignity into the slime of dishonorable passions, and became like the wild beasts. Reading history and seeing contemporary reality, one shudders and is ashamed of mankind's horrible crimes and shameful acts. Among the billions of people, however, there are still some who, by their acts and virtues, have honored and continue to honor humanity, demonstrating that we were created for a higher purpose, making us aspire for heaven, for the blessed life which man lived in Paradise before the Fall.

If someone should ask which human being of all the billions of human beings who have lived on earth, reached the highest point of moral grandeur, in other words, who is the greatest of all Saints, we would answer not on our own authority, but would give the answer of the Church, which is the pillar and ground of the truth (II Tim. 3:15). Our Church, having the Holy Scriptures as a foundation, answers that, after Christ, who is not a mere man, but the God-Man and a Saint in the absolute sense, comes a woman. She is the All-Holy Virgin Mary.

The Virgin Mary, by God's grace and through her virtues, came to such a high state of holiness, that she surpassed not only every human being, but even the angels and the archangels. The spiritual height and depth of the Virgin, to use the words of the Akathist Hymn, are unattainable: "Hail Height insurmountable for the human mind; Hail Depth inexplorable to angelic eye."

The Virgin, as our Church praises her, is "more honorable than the Cherubim and incomparably more glorious than the Seraphim." If mankind is a miracle of divine creation, then the Virgin Mary is the most exceptional miracle of divine grace.

From the moment when the first woman, Eve, sinned and carried mankind along with her into the abyss of calamity, centuries and millenia had passed. In the midst of this terrible darkness, one hope warmed souls, namely, that the situation would one day be radically different. The ancient prophecy, the first prophecy after the Fall of the First Man and First Woman, the *First Gospel* as it was called, spoke about a woman, a woman whose son would fight and defeat satan, and would give the world new life. From careful study of this prophecy, it is apparent that this woman would not give birth in the usual way women give birth. This woman would give birth without knowing man. She would bear as a virgin. This prophecy about the virgin is repeated more precisely and with different symbols in the Old Testament. The Book of Isaiah gives the clearest prophecy: "Behold, a virgin shall conceive in the womb, and shall bring forth a son, and his name shall be called Emmanuel" (Isaiah 7:14). Eight hundred years before the star of Bethlehem shone, Isaiah saw the Virgin and her son Emmanuel.

The Virgin gave birth to her only-begotten son, our Lord, Jesus Christ. But how did the Virgin give birth? Unbelievers of every century have argued against this and will contine to do so. What do we answer? We say: "Which is a greater miracle – a Virgin to give birth or the world to be created from nothing?" Certainly, the greater is the creation of the universe from nothing, and if this greater one took place, why not a lesser miracle, the Virgin Birth?

The all-holy Mother of God was a virgin before giving birth, during birth, and remained a virgin after giving birth. Our holy Lady is ever-virgin. Our Church preaches this as a revealed truth, and we proclaim this truth each time we recite the Symbol of Faith, saying: "and was incarnated by the Holy Spirit and of the Virgin Mary, and became man."

We Orthodox do not deify the Virgin, as some heretics like Protestants and Jehovah's Witnesses accuse us. We do not believe that the Virgin is a Goddess, but we say that the Virgin is superior to the angels, and that is why we call her Most Holy — that God selected the Most holy Mother in order to take flesh and be born. For this reason we call her Theotokos, God-birthgiver. Because of her exceptional virtues she is the perfect example of Woman.

But while the Holy Scriptures and the Church in its teaching elevate the Virgin to ineffable heights, and angels and archangels bow before her, we have in our country many nominal Christians who open their foul mouths and blaspheme her worse than heretics and unbelievers!

Dear Christians, let us all fight to stop this blasphemy and save ourselves from God's wrath.

THE SACRIFICE

*". . . Crucified for our salvation under Pontius Pilate,
He suffered and was buried."*

Dear friends, our Lord Jesus Christ Himself said: "the Son of man came not to be ministered unto, but to minister, and to give his life as a ransom for many" (Matt 20:28). That is to say, he did not come to be served as the ancient kings were served by their many subjects, but unlike the great and powerful people of this world, He came to become a servant, a slave of all men. Christ, the King of kings and Lord of lords, who governs the entire material and spiritual universe, before whom angels and archangels tremble, left all His glory and appeared on earth as a man, a very poor and insignificant man. No one could ever imagine that, under this lowly image in which Christ appeared, *God was hidden.* Even the devil was mistaken and became a captive. Like the fish that sees a lure and does not suspect that there is a fish-hook beneath it, so it was with the devil. He saw a man with flesh and bones like any other man, and he thought he could easily defeat Him as he did countless other men. But in the end he faced the tremendous power of the Christ, the son of the Virgin, the Son of God as well. Hades was defeated.

Christ served humanity more than any other person. His earthly life was one of continuous service, continuous sacrifice. The Apostle Peter, who followed Him closely and knew the details of His earthly life, said that Christ "went about doing good" (Acts 10:38)). This means that Christ spent His whole life giving the world the light of His teaching, doing good to His friends and enemies alike. Yes, His entire life was one continuous sacrifice.

To give an example, imagine, dear friends, a ladder with its top in the stars, a ladder with countless rungs, the bottom one being on earth. Imagine someone descending on that ladder, down to the last rung, that on the earth. This is an image of the *humiliation*, the sacrifice which Christ made. Christ came down to this earth from the heavenly heights, lived and walked like a poor and insignificant person, and in this way He served and helped mankind. And descending the rungs of humiliation, He reached the last one, on which He was crucified. Christ's crucifixion is the deepest humiliation, the greatest sacrifice offered to humanity, surpassing any other sacrifice – an Infinite Sacrifice!

Mankind was well acquainted with sacrifice. It knew of people who were sacrificed for the good of their fellows. One such sacrifice is that of the ancient king of Athens, Codros. Codros saw that the people of his kingdom could not be saved unless he himself would be sacrificed. He left his palace, took off his royal garments and, dressed like a peasant, went out of the city which was under enemy seige. His enemies captured and killed him, and in this way he caused the seige to end and saved the city.

The sacrifice of Codros, however, as well as all those of any noble heroes for the good of their fellows, cannot be compared to the voluntary sacrifice of the God-Man, Christ on Golgotha. This is because those were sacrifices of men for men, but the sacrifice of Golgotha was a sacrifice of the God-Man for men. Their sacrifices saved only a few people from bodily danger, but the sacrifice of Christ saved all humanity from the greatest danger, the danger of spiritual perdition from sin. He liberated the human race from guilt and the curse. He reconciled God and mankind. He united heaven and earth, extending worldly and supernatural gifts, and granting grace like an inexhaustible river everywhere, throughout all time to every generation.

Christ is the salvation, the peace and the hope of the whole world. What Christ did for mankind no other sacrifice could have done – no other heroic deed done by the children of man can match it.

These are not empty words, but a reality which all those who believe in Christ actually feel in their hearts. Human beings, angels, and archangels did not save us, but Christ: To Him is due all honor and glory forever.

The world's salvation by the precious Blood of Christ is an event of universal importance, an event-mystery. Human reason cannot comprehend how Christ's Blood became a ransom for humanity. This event, a hidden mystery of divine wisdom, before the Gospel was written, before it had been proclaimed everywhere as an article of the Symbol of the Faith, this event was prophesied centuries before. Anyone reading the Psalms, the Prophecies would think that those God-inspired writers, who lived 800 and 1000 years before Christ, were actually present at the Crucifixion and heard and saw what took place. But of all the prophecies, we will mention only one, that famous prophecy of Isaiah, which is read at the Service of the Sixth Hour on Great Friday. Isaiah, describing the Christ says: "He bears our sins, and is pierced for us; yet we accounted him to be in trouble, and suffering and in affliction. But He was wounded on account of our sins, and was bruised because of our iniquities: the chastisement of our peace was upon him; and by his bruises we were healed. All we as sheep have gone astray; every one has gone astray in his way; and the Lord gave him up for our sins. And he, despite his affliction, opens not his mouth" (Isaiah 53:4-7).

This is only one part of Isaiah's prophecy, which, because of its importance, is read twice on Great Friday. We will not try to explain the whole prophecy, but we recommend to those who are young and have a good memory to open the Holy Scriptures, find this chapter, learn it by heart, and say it like a hymn of the Crucifixion to remember Christ's Passion with thanksgiving. "He bears our sins. . . ."

Christ was crucified, sacrificed for the salvation and life of the world. He offered Himself as a blameless sacrifice, which is continued through the Mystery of Holy Eucharist. But, how do we know that this sacrifice was accepted by the Heavenly Father? Proof is offered by His Resurrection, His Ascension into heaven, Pentecost and twenty centuries of Christianity, a history of miracles!

To Christ, the Redeemer of our souls, belong glory, honor and thanksgiving, now and forever.

With these few and meager words, dear friends, we have tried to explain articles 4 through 7 of the Symbol of the Faith.

THE HOLY SPIRIT

"And I believe in the Holy Spirit, the Lord, the Giver of Life, who proceeds from the Father, who, together with the Father and the Son, is worshipped and glorified; who spoke through the Prophets."

And now, in the eighth article of the Symbol of the Faith, we will speak about the holy Spirit. But how can we tell or understand the *kerygma* (teaching) about the holy Spirit?

Unfortunately, we live in a time when material things absorb the attention of everyone, everyone speaks about worldly things and is only interested in these things. People have become materialistic – matter oriented, like moles, who always live underground and cannot understand that on the surface of the earth there are so many beautiful things. Modern people are moles. They live and work in the endless tunnels of worldly existence and have extinguished the idea that above the material world there is a spiritual one, that above matter there exists spirit; and for this reason, when people hear that there is a Holy Spirit, they react like one hearing a foreign language. Even we, the preachers of the Gospel, are not on the lofty level of the Church Fathers who spoke for hours about the Holy Spirit. A general spiritual collapse has occurred today, both of preachers and listeners.

O Holy Spirit, who enlightened the fishermen of Galilee, come again into our midst. Sit in our hearts, open the hidden ears of our souls to hear Your sounds, and give us Gospel preachers of the twentieth century strength to preach Your wonders!

Holy Spirit! As heretics appeared in ancient times rejecting the divinity of Christ, so heretics appeared who did not accept the divinity of the Holy Spirit, saying the Holy Spirit was not God. These heretics were called the pneumatomachs or Macedonianists after their leader, Macedonios. The modern, so-called Jehovah's Witnesses are also horrible Pneumatomachs.

The person who rejects the Holy Spirit rejects Christ, the Holy Trinity, and will come to a point where he will believe in some vague superpower. And moving from rejection to rejection, he will end in complete atheism and unbelief.

The Holy Spirit is not an attribute or energy of God, but is a Being, and Person, an Hypostasis, as are the Father and the Son. As the Symbol of the Faith declares, "the Lord, the Giver of Life, who proceeds from the Father, who together with the Father and the Son, is worshipped and glorified; Who spoke through the Prophets."

Many passages from Holy Scripture testify that the Holy Spirit is a Person, equal to the Father and Son, that is to say, He is God. We will not mention all of them, only three passages.

The first quotation about the Holy Spirit is found in our Lord's farewell speech, which He gave to His disciples on Great Thursday after the Last Supper. He said: "If ye love me, keep my commandments. And I will pray the Father, and He shall give you another Comforter, that he may abide with you forever; even the Spirit of truth; whom the world cannot receive, because it seeth him not, neither knoweth him; but ye know him; for he dwelleth with you, and shall be in you. I will not leave you comfortless" (John 14:15-18). He said: Dear disciples, don't be sad that I am now leaving this earthly life. You will not be like orphans, you will not be deprived of a person to give you comfort and courage in the struggle. You will have the Holy Spirit; the Father will give Him to you...."

In this passage, the Holy Spirit is clearly defined. Christ is a Comforter, and so is the Holy Spirit; Christ is God, the Holy Spirit is God.

The second quotation comes from the message of Christ before His ascension into heaven: "Go ye and teach all nations, baptizing them in the name of the Father, and of the Son, and of the Holy Spirit" (Matt. 28:19). In this quotation we see that the Holy Spirit is on the same level with the Father and Son, because like the Father and Son, the Holy Spirit is God. The three are of the same essence and have the same honor. None of them is superior or inferior to the others.

The third quotation is the last verse of the Second Epistle of St. Paul to the Corinthians: "The grace of the Lord Jesus Christ, the love of God, and the communion of the Holy Spirit be with you all" (II Cor. 13:13). This passage is said during the Divine Liturgy, as an apostolic blessing, after the reading of the Creed. And in this quotation, it appears clearly that the Holy Spirit is equal with God the Father and the Lord Jesus Christ, one of the three Persons of the Deity.

How are the three persons one God? We answered this question previously and said that the teaching of the

Holy Trinity is Christianity's greatest mystery. It is not possible for our little minds to comprehend it, but our hearts believe it and our lips confess it. St. Athanasios the Great, who theologized much on this great mystery, said: "The Father is the source, the Son is the river, and the Holy Spirit is the water which we drink."

The grace of the Holy Spirit, like rich and fresh water, is in the Church, and whoever wants this water, approaches and takes this immortal water, some more, some less. A small vessel holds little water; a large one, much. It is like this with the grace of the Holy Spirit. There have been Saints in the Church, who, by faith, good intention, and purity of life, became precious, selected vessels of the holy Spirit.

The Holy Spirit is present in the Church. Whatever a chosen and holy person of the Church has to offer is a fruit of the Holy Spirit. When prophets and apostles prophesied and taught, when priests celebrate the holy Mysteries, when zealot preachers teach the word of God and draw souls to God, when souls repent and kneel before the Crucifix and ask forgiveness from their Father Confessor, when there are gatherings of hierarchs or laymen to discuss the Kingdom of God, when a tear of repentance is shed or a sigh is heard, when a pure thought, wish, or act takes place, there the Holy Spirit is.

Therefore, let us sinners of the earth glorify the Holy Spirit, and let us proclaim our faith by saying: "I believe...in the Holy Spirit, the Lord, the Giver of Life, Who proceeds from the Father, Who together with the Father and the Son is worshipped and glorified; Who spoke through the Prophets."

THE CHURCH

"I believe in One, Holy, Catholic and Apostolic Church."

The Symbol of our Faith is like an architectural work – everything was placed where it is with purpose and skill. Every word, even the word "and," was placed with a holy wisdom. The words are connected to each other in such a way that if one word or letter is added or taken away, the entire structure of the Faith is shaken. It is for this reason the Church chants of the Symbol of the Faith:

"When these preachers of Christ received the whole spiritual radiance of the Holy Spirit, the supernatural revelation, they spoke of it with brevity and much wisdom, divinely inspired, the blessed ones setting forth evangelical doctrines and pious traditions. Having received the revelation of these from above, they expounded with clarity and in a state of illumination and divinely taught faith."

As we have said in previous homilies, there is a marvelous order in the fundamental teachings of our Faith. The dogma about the existence of God the Father comes first. The dogma about the existence of the Son of God and His plan for the salvation of the world comes next, i.e. that the Second Person of the holy Trinity came down to earth, took on flesh from the Virgin Mary, was crucified, resurrected and ascended into heaven and will come again to judge the world. Then comes the teaching about the Holy Spirit, the Third Person of the Holy

Trinity. After this is the teaching about the Church. Here is the fitting place for the Church, because if Christ were not crucified and resurrected, if He did not send the Holy Spirit from heaven, the Church would not exist.

The Fathers delved into the teaching about the Church and observed that, as Eve came out of Adam's side, the Church came out of the side of the new Adam, Christ, Whose side, opened by the soldier's spear, issued forth blood and water. Water is the symbol of Holy Baptism and Blood symbolizes Holy Communion. The Church is based primarily on Christ's sacrifice and is enlivened by the Holy Spirit, Who came on the day of Pentecost. Pentecost is the fulfillment of Christ's promise and the birthday of the Church.

The Church is not a benevolent institution to deal out charity to people. It is a structure which has been instituted by God's benevolence. *God created an eternal institution.* All the dark powers of the world were not able to destroy the Church and never will.

What is the purpose of the Church? It has the highest of all purposes, over those of any other institution, be it government, state, kingdom, school or university. The purpose of the Church is to continue the redemptive work of Christ to the end of the Age. In other words, the purpose of the Church is the *sanctification of souls.* Sanctification has two sides: one is deliverance from the guilt of sin. No matter how much unbelievers insist that there is no sin and that we should not be troubled by the "bugbear" of sin, sin is a cruel reality. Moments come to unbelievers when they confess the existence and power of sin, and they are shaken. Some of them go into despair and commit suicide. Sin presses against people's breast like a heavy stone, and it is from this oppressive weight that Christ frees people. He says to every sinner who believes and repents: "My child, your sins are forgiven" (Matt. 9:2).

Deliverance from sin, as we have said, is one side of the sanctification that takes place in the Church. The other side gives the believer power to fight and defeat his evil and corrupt nature, his wickedness and passion, so that he can progress spiritually. This power is given through the Mysteries of the Church, especially Holy Communion. The Church is the Treasury of Divine Grace and the laboratory of holiness. She takes the worst sinners and changes them into saints, because the Church is armed with all the means necessary to spiritually transform and perfect humanity. Within the Church, mankind meets its destiny.

The Church is security, sanctification and salvation – the Church is spiritual glory.

The Church is not only clergy; it is also laity, men and women, young and old, everybody who has been baptized according to the orthodox canons and precepts. The Church is not only the faithful living here, but it is also the faithful who have passed away and are living as spirits in the other life. The Church on earth is called *militant* and the Church in heaven is called *triumphant*. The angels also belong to the Church.

This Church is the beautiful Bride, and Christ is the Groom of the Church. The Church, in other words, is the Kingdom of God, the "blessed kingdom of the Father, Son and Holy Spirit."

As the Symbol of the Faith proclaims, the Church is "one," because the true Faith is one. All other faiths are heresy and in error. The Church is "holy" because Her character and mission are holy. The Church is "catholic" because Her purpose is to include all the world within Her bosom. Finally, the Church is "apostolic" because whatever She teaches is not a novelty, but the teachings of the God-inspired Apostles.

The Church which has all these earmarks is the Orthodox Catholic Church. She, then, is the true Church which Christ established, and in this Church we are born, baptized and live. And when we end our temporal life, we will enjoy heaven's glory.

BAPTISM

"I acknowledge one baptism for the remission of sins."

This tenth article of the Symbol of the Faith, dear readers, speaks about Baptism.

Some say: We know that the Orthodox Church has seven Sacraments. They are Baptism, Chrismation, Holy Eucharist, Confession, Ordination, Marriage, and Holy Unction. Divine Grace acts through these Sacraments, having an inexhaustible source in Christ's sacrifice on the Cross. It is from this sacrifice that the seven Sacraments (Mysteries) derive their power. In the Orthodox Church there is a fountain with seven spouts, with seven pipes which all get their immortal water of Divine Grace from Christ's sacrifice on the Cross. Why, then, in the Creed's tenth article is only Holy Baptism mentioned?

We reply: Just because this article does not mention any of the other Sacraments does not mean they are underestimated or are not recognized as Sacraments, as heretics maintain. On the contrary, there are seven Sacraments, but in the Symbol of Faith, only Baptism is mentioned, because in the order of Sacraments, Baptism is the first which a Christian receives when he enters Christianity. The Church is a magnificent edifice, but to enter it, one must go through the main door, then he can see all the places and storeys within. The main door through which one enters the Divine Edifice, the Church, is to become a Christian through Baptism.

But, someone else may ask: "What good is Baptism?"

We answer, every person born into this world does not come into it clean and pure from his mother's womb. On every human being is a grave hereditary wound, stemming from an ancient wound. The Church calls it ancestral sin, the first sin which mankind committed, i.e. Adam and Eve, when they disobeyed God's command. From that time on, as if from an infected fountain, humanity's sinfulness begins. As happens when a reservoir is infected, all the water in people's homes supplied by the reservoir is also infected, so it is with all human beings, who come from the same couple who sinned – they are infected with that same sin.

That people born after Adam and Eve are infected with sin is evident by the fact that people, wherever they live, consider themselves sinners and guilty. They groan and attempt to redeem themselves from evil. In ancient times, the people worshipped idols, they went even to the extreme of sacrificing other people. They thought that with the blood of animals or people their sins would be washed away. Even today in India, one sees millions of people going to wash themselves in the great River Ganges, believing that its waters have the power to wash away sin.

But neither washing in the Ganges, nor the sacrifices of Jews of pagan peoples have power to save people from sin. All that is needed is an admission on a person's part that he is a sinner and guilty.

Let us thank and glorify God because, where sacrifices of the ancient world did not succeed, the sacrifice of Christ on the Cross did. As we have said, one drop of Christ's sinless Blood is enough to wipe away all the sins of mankind, and this cleansing, i.e.

forgiveness of sins, which is derived from Christ's Cross is given to mankind in the dispensible form of Baptism in the Name of Christ. Christ said it clearly and it is above dispute: "He that believeth and is baptized shall be saved" (Mark 16:16).

After His resurrection, Christ sent His disciples to preach, and He commanded them to baptize those who believe in the Name of the Father, Son and Holy Spirit.

St. Paul speaks especially about Baptism in his Epistle to the Romans. He says that two things take place during Baptism: one is the Crucifixion; the other, the Resurrection. One is death; the other, life. How does this happen? Let's explain:

We are sinners and deserve death. We should be crucified, but instead of us, Christ was crucified and died. He was crucified not because he was a sinner, but for the sins of the whole world. So now, when we are submerged into the water, it is like being crucified and dying with Christ. In Baptism, as it takes place in the Orthodox Church, one is completely submerged into the Baptismal Font, representing Christ's crucifixion. When the baptized person comes out of the water, freed of the taint of sin, that moment is like coming out of a grave, leaving death and decay behind and beginning a new life. The Orthodox Baptism gives a vivid representation of Christ's Crucifixion and Resurrection. St. Paul teaches: "For surely you know that when we were baptized into union with Christ Jesus, we were baptized into union with his death. By our baptism then, we were buried with him and shared his death, in order that, just as Christ was raised from death by the glorious power of the Father, so also we might live a new life" (Rom. 6:3-4).

The things that take place during Baptism are great and wonderful. But, unfortunately, most of us do not feel this. We are ignorant of the Sacrament, and everything takes place as a formality, without the awe of God and consciousness of what is taking place. If a leprous person were baptized and came out of the Font clean, or if a dead person were baptized and came to life, then everyone would marvel. But these cases would be small miracles compared to what does take place during Baptism. Our souls go in leprous and come out pure and clean, and we are truly alive.

Truly great and wondrous are the things you do in Your Church, O Lord!

THE RESURRECTION OF THE DEAD

"I await the resurrection of the dead. . ."

If mankind had never sinned, dear readers, we would never have known death; we would have remained immortal — immortal not only in soul, but also in body. But sin occurred, and along with the other consequences, it brought this calamity called death, which is the separation of soul and body. This is the punishment we received after committing sin. "Dust thou art, and unto dust shalt thou return" (Gen. 3:19). The body, made up of different natural elements, moves and acts by means of the immortal soul. The soul now loses its precious companion with death, which dies and dissolves into the elements from which it was made. The flesh decays and only bones remain, and even these, over a long period of time, wear away and become ashes, reminding us of the Church hymn: "I called to mind the Prophet who cried, 'I am but earth and ash.'"

All bodies rot away and dissolve. However, there are some exceptions to this natural law of decay: the holy *relics* of men and women who were sanctified. These bodies remain incorrupt and are proof of the power of Christ, who works miracles through the relics of Saints.

Now the Church, in the eleventh article of the Symbol of the Faith, proclaims that the dead will be resurrected. *Will* they be resurrected? No! shout unbelievers. But what are their arguments?

The bodies of human beings, they say, dissolve into the great crucible of the earth, and only their ashes exist. What about bodies burned in terrible fires, bodies of people drowned in the great seas and eaten by fish, bodies of people devoured by lions and other wild beasts – how is it possible to resurrect these bodies?

In Christ's time, there were people who believed in God, but did not believe that bodies would be resurrected. These people were the Sadducees. When St. Paul went to Athens, stood on the Areopagus and preached that a day will come when the dead will rise and be judged, the philosophers listening to him began to laugh and mocked him. Today there are still many who do not believe in the resurrection of the dead. They say:

"When someone dies, forget him, he's gone for good!"

In spite of this, the Church continues to say that the dead will be resurrected. Where do we find the truth about the resurrection? Primarily, in God's word. Even the wisest people can be mistaken, but the word of God is truth; and since the word of God declares that the dead will rise, we believe it and proclaim it.

Where in God's word, the Holy Scriptures, is the resurrection of the dead mentioned? Let's bring up only some of these passages:

First, the famous 36th chapter of the prophecy of Ezekiel. Ezekiel saw an awesome vision. He was brought to a field where, many years before, a battle had taken place and many people were killed. Their bodies were eaten by wild birds and their fleshless bones covered the plain. The spectacle was horrible. While the prophet looked at the scattered bones in this macabre scene, he heard a voice say to him:

"Son of man, is there any hope for these bones to live?"

"O Lord, Thou knowest," he answered.

"Prophesy to these bones," the voice of God commanded.

The prophet obeyed the order and prophesied to the bones. Immediately, the bones began to creak and come together, joining one to another, making whole skeletons. The skeletons filled with flesh and were finally covered with skin. But they were still dead bodies; there was no life in them — an endless array of dead bodies.

"Prophesy again," commanded the voice of God.

The prophet spoke again and wind came from the four corners of the earth and the dead bodies stood up on their feet and walked as if in a military parade. This vision is proof, an assurance of God, that the dead shall be resurrected. They will be resurrected by the trumpet of the archangel, which will sound by God's command — the trumpet call of resurrection for all the dead.

Another quotation related to the resurruction of the dead is found in the Second Book of Maccabees. There we have the story of seven brothers, and their heroic mother. In spite of all the threats made them by a tyrant, they did not deny their true faith, but with the courage their faith gave them, they faced their martyrdom. Although the tyrant tortured them; cutting off their hands and feet, these admirable martyrs answered the tyrant:

". . . Hands and feet are not ours. God gave them to us, and we believe that God, for whom we are sacrificed, will give them back to us in the resurrection!"

Christ Himself assured us in the most positive way that the dead will be resurrected. We hear Christ's words in the Funeral Service when the Gospel is read, saying, "Verily, verily, I say unto you, the hour is coming, and now is, when the dead shall hear the voice of the Son of God, and they that hear it shall live" (John 5:25).

In addition, Christ proclaimed the resurrection of the dead through miracles. He raised dead people three times: the daughter of Jairus, the son of the widow of Nain, and Lazarus, who was dead four days. Finally, the greatest proof of the resurrection of the dead is Christ's own resurrection.

By Christ's resurrection death was completely defeated; and believers of every century proclaim with the Apostle Paul: "O Death, where is thy sting? O grave, where thy victory?" (I Cor. 15:55).

Yes, dear friends, the dead will be resurrected, and we ourselves will be resurrected, because, after a while we too will be dead.

But the question is raised: "How will bodies be resurrected from the dead?" To this question St. Paul gives an answer. He gives examples, and one example is the seed of plants. What is the importance of a seed? It is sown in the earth, buried like a dead person. It rots like a dead body, and out of this rotten seed comes a sweet-smelling flower, which, with its new appearance proclaims that God makes new bodies from dead ones, bright bodies which will differ from the old ones as much as a huge oak tree differs from a tiny acorn.

O God, Thou dost great and marvelous wonders in heaven and earth!

Let everyone of us, with steadfast faith, proclaim: "I await the resurrection of the dead."

BEYOND THE GRAVE

". . .And life in the ages to come."

In the last article of the Symbol of the Faith we proclaim that another life exists beyond the grave, which is eternal. Let's speak about it now.

Everybody dies. Death is the punishment given us because of sin. Death, however, as we discussed it in our previous homily, is not annihilation of our human existence. The shovel of the grave digger does not mean that there, in the grave, is the end of us. Death marks a turning point in human life, just as birth does. This phase of our life is not the last one; it is the beginning of a new life under different conditions.

Our Church teaches that we are composed of two things — body and soul. The body decays after death and dissolves into the elements from which it is made. "Dust thou art, and unto dust shalt thou return" (Gen. 3:19). One day, however, our bodies will be resurrected, spiritual and incorruptible.

The soul, though, does not consist of material elements, as does the body. It is immaterial, and being immaterial it is immortal. The soul does not die, it lives on earth together with the body and uses the body as a servant. With death, this union is interrupted and the soul alone, free from the weights and responsibilities of the flesh, continues living, but under other conditions.

The souls of the departed await the terrible Day of Judgement, and those who on earth lived according to the will of God have a foretaste of heaven, experiencing joy and gladness; but those who did not live as God wanted, who remained unrepentant until the end of their lives, experience sorrow and distress. They feel beforehand a measure of eternal damnation, and, like a defendant on trial, having committed many crimes and not at peace, but in agony over the outcome of the trial, so also are the sinful and unrepentant souls who are waiting for the Day of Judgement. This state, which will last from the day of their death to the Day of Universal Judgement, is called the *Intermediate State* of souls.

The Intermediate State will come to an end. The Day of Universal Judgement will come and then, as the Lord assures us, people will be separated: some "shall go away into everlasting punishment," and others "into eternal life" (Matt. 25:46).

Eternal life, eternal damnation! People today hear these words and do not pay attention, because they do not believe in God, or, if they believe, think that it is impossible for God, who is Love, to punish people this way.

There is no Hell, they say, there is no eternal life. We shall not bring in here philosophical arguments to convince people that there is a Hell and a Paradise. Since Christ in a most positive way assured us that Hell and Paradise exist, we believe Christ, Who never lies. Christ is the Truth and Life — if we do not believe Christ, whom shall we believe? Christ is the truthful witness, and His witness is worth more than that of people. Only Christ knows our past, present and future. Outside of Christ, we do not know what life is and what death is.

Eternal life! Eternal life differs greatly from our present life, because our present life is transient, that is, it lasts only a little time, while life beyond the grave has no end. The 80 or 90 years we might live here on earth, compared to eternal life, are only a drop of water in the ocean.

A certain author, in order to give an idea of what eternity is like, used this example. Imagine, he says, that all the sand from every river, lake and sea were all in one place. Then imagine a bird coming to take one grain of sand in its beak. After a thousand years, another comes and takes a second grain of sand, and this continues every thousand years. How many millions, trillions of years must pass before the birds take the last grain? No matter if it seems impossible! The mathematicians say the time will come when a bird will take the last grain from this pile of sand and there will be an end; but in the eternity about which Christ speaks, there will be no end.

The life we speak of is not only eternal, it is also unchangeable. That is, the decisions the supreme tribunal of God pronounces for unbelievers and unrepenting sinners cannot be changed.

Some may ask: "What is Hell." Is it snakes and scorpions? Fire and brimstone? Darkness without light? It is something worse than these, something worse than anyone cold imagine. Hell, for one thing, is a sinner's conscience, which now, in the heart of the impious, the criminal, the murderer, is dormant. In the other world, however, it will awaken, and one will see all the crimes he has committed. One will see the whole tragic situation, and he will hear the terrible, endless "I accuse," addressed to the guilty.

"What is Paradise?" It is a new life so beautiful the human mind cannot imagine. There, none of the sufferings exist which bother us here. There is no sickness or death, derision or slander, cries or mourning. New bodies, glorious and incorruptible will be resurrected, differing from the old, earthly bodies as a flower differs from a bare seed, as an oak differs from an acorn. We will have new, spiritual bodies, like the body of Christ after his resurrection. There will be a new union with the soul, which, united with the spiritual body, will enjoy the blessings which human eye cannot see, nor human ear hear, nor human heart imagine.

Paradise! An illustrious old preacher used to say, we will enjoy you (Paradise), but here we cannot understand you!

Eternal Damnation, Eternal Life! There is life in the Age to come, and the kind of life we will live then depends on the kind of life we live now.

O Christ, Enlighten us to believe and not lose everything, and then lament in vain.

SAINT BASIL THE GREAT

V

COMMEMORATIONS
(THE *ANAPHORA*)

LET US STAND ARIGHT

*"Let us stand aright; let us stand in awe; let us attend,
that we may make the Holy Offering in peace."*

Following the "Creed," dear friends, which all the communicants should recite, we say "Amen." Here, "Amen" has an affirmative meaning, that is, the dogmas (truths) which the Symbol of the Faith contains are all real, all true, and whatever is said and is not in accord with the Symbol of the Faith is heresy and error. All who believe and live according to these fundamental truths of the Symbol of the Faith are fortunate.

May the "Creed" be our life-long companion; may we never doubt what it teaches, and when we come to the end of our lives, may the "Creed" be our last words. On the Cyclade islands, when someone is about to die, it is customary for a friend to kneel near the deathbed and recite the "Creed." This implies that the soul leaving this world is not an unbelieving soul, but one that believes in the Triune God, and that it is going beyond this life of grace hoping in God's mercy.

After the "Amen," which should be said aloud not only by the cantor, but by all the people, the deacon or priest addresses the following exhortation: "Let us stand aright; let us stand in awe; let us attend, that we may make the holy offering in peace." With this command we enter the most sacred part of the Divine Liturgy, which is the consecration of the precious gifts, the celebration of the Mystery of the Divine Eucharist. Everything which preceded was an introduction to this main part of the Divine Liturgy.

Having in mind an older interpretation of the Divine Liturgy, we will try to explain the exhortation, "Let us stand aright; let us stand in awe...."

The world which God created is visible and invisible. The visible world consists of rivers, seas, mountains, trees, plants, stars and mankind. But man is both visible and invisible. He is visible in body, but has an invisible soul. Mankind is the link between the material and spiritual worlds.

There are, however, other beings, higher than us, which do not have bodies like ours. They have etherial bodies. They move easily, carrying out God's commands, protecting human beings. They live near God and continuously sing "Holy, holy, holy, Lord of Hosts, heaven and earth are full of Thy glory" (Isaiah 6:3). These are angels.

Angels exist. Many Scripture passages assure us of this. Reason also accepts it — just think: Did not God, who created so many creatures, also have the power to create other beings, incorporeal in nature? God's power is limitless.

Angels are innumerable. They form orders and legions. Among these are the archangels Michael, Gabriel and Raphael. They are also called the Commanders.

Besides these three archangels, there was once another archangel. Because he was so brilliant, he was called "Lucifer." But this archangel, as the Prophet Isaiah says (14:12), did not remain faithful and devoted to God. He fell from his high position because of his pride.

Lucifer was proud. He said, "I will place my throne above the stars; I will become superior to God!" As soon as he began thinking haughtily, he started to fall from his height of glory, into the abyss. His form changed; he became satan. Having fallen from heaven, he carried away with him a great many angels who made up his legion. This is not a lie, it is not a fairy-tale, but a terrible event which took place in the heavenly world; an event testified to by Christ Himself, who said: "I saw Satan fall like lightening from heaven" (Luke 10:18). The moment Lucifer fell, taking with him a multitude of angels, the archangel Michael with his angelic trumpet heralded the other angels: "Let us stand aright!"

That which the archangel Michael commanded then, at the tragic fall of Lucifer, the priest of the supreme God commands us now: "Let us stand aright!"

"Let us stand aright." That angelic command must ever resound in our ears, for as long as we are in this world, filled with temptation and scandal, demons and mankind will not stop tempting us to do evil.

"Let us stand aright." It is an angelic voice, the inspired voice of the Apostle Paul, who says: "Work out your own salvation with fear and trembling" (Phil. 2:12). It is the voice of Christ Himself: "Watch and pray, that ye enter not into temptation" (Matt. 26:41).

But if there is any time the command "Let us stand aright" should be heard with more regard, it is the moment when the priest is preparing to offer the Mystery of Holy Eucharist.

"Let us stand aright." That is, our position at this time should be one of a Christian who feels that something inconceivably great is about to happen – the miracle which changes the bread and wine into the Body and Blood of Christ. If someone is seated at this moment, he should stand up, and there standing, should hear this part of the Liturgy. The soul as well as the body should be in a standing position. The Christian must be careful not to be carried away by worldly, vain thoughts, which throw him down and make his soul drag along when it should be flying in the heights like a golden eagle, making circles around the sacred and mysterious sacrifice.

"Let us stand aright; let us stand in awe; let us attend, that we may make the holy offering in peace." The Mystery is called a holy Offering (Anaphora) because we are led upwards; we ascend, and peace must prevail. No sinful thoughts, no thoughts of hate or revenge should trouble us at this time.

The Holy Eucharist is also called the "sacrifice of peace" and "sacrifice of praise," because with the precious Blood of Christ, heaven and earth have been reconciled, sinful man with the heavenly Father, and we therefore give praise and thanks to God from the bottom of our hearts, and for this reason, after "Let us stand aright," we hear: "A mercy of peace, a sacrifice of praise."

THE APOSTOLIC BLESSING

The Divine Liturgy, dear readers, moves along. We are almost at the climax – glory be to God! The summit of the Divine Liturgy is that sacred moment when the bread and wine become the Body and Blood of Christ. This is the miracle which takes place in the Liturgy, and those who believe in Christ sense this.

Because the sacred moment of the miracle is approaching, the celebrating priest calls the faithful to strain their attention, to stay all the more with the awesome things that are said and done, to stand devoutly, having love and forgiveness in their hearts.

The unbeliever should stay away along with all those holding hatred and seeking revenge! A sacrifice is offered, a sacrifice of praise, love and peace.

Immediately after the cantors sing: "A mercy of peace, a sacrifice of praise," the celebrating priest comes out before the Beautiful Gate and blesses the people, saying "The grace of our Lord Jesus Christ, and the love of God the Father and the communion of the Holy Spirit be with you all."

Let us try to explain these words.

We should know first of all that these words are from Holy Scripture. They are found at the end of II Corinthians (13:13). It is a *blessing* which Paul, the great Apostle to the Gentiles, sends *to his spiritual children*, the Christians of the city of Corinth.

How he labored for them! He converted them from idolatry to Christianity, and these Christians constituted a small minority in the large population of idolaters in the big city. These few were fighting the great fight, a double fight, protecting themselves from sin and bringing other idolaters to Christ. Paul did not want any of his spiritual children to be defeated in this spiritual struggle, but wanted them to be victorious internally and externally. He wanted them to defeat both sin (which shakes every human heart) and the pagan world around them, and so he desired with all his heart that the grace of Christ, the love of the Father and the communion of the Holy Spirit be with them.

What priceless gifts! When these three are in the hearts of us Christians, we are invincible. No one is able to defeat us. We will be burning spirits and not flesh and blood!

But what is the grace of Christ, what is the love of the Father, and what is the communion of the Holy Spirit?

The grace of our Lord Jesus Christ: instead of another opinion, let us give an example which gives a faint idea of what grace means, although we hear it many times in church. Let us suppose that a certain man committed a crime and was sentenced to death. While the convict was confined in prison, waiting for his execution, the Governor of the State suddenly gives him a pardon. The convict is not executed, his life is spared.

We spoke in a parable, dear friends. Every sinner is a convict, having committed many sins, great and small; he is condemned to eternal death, separation from God, the fountain of every good thing. The sinner-convict lives a miserable life. Divine wrath hangs over the sinner's head by a slender thread. But while the sinner is in this terrible situation, grace comes from Christ. It comes from Christ's sacrifice on the cross. Yes, there on the cross, the royal decree of grace was signed, forgiving all the sins of the world. *We are no longer convicts, but free men.* We are not only free, but grace, in addition to forgiving our sins, gives the repentant believer the mysterious power to conquer sin.

The grace of our Lord Jesus Christ and the love of the Father...! But what is this *love of the Father*?

God, the heavenly Father, loves us. One might ask: What did we do to deserve this love? We are sinners, unclean and impious, worthy of condemnation. We are God's enemies. In spite of this, the heavenly Father loves us! He loves us, though we cannot offer Him anything except our sins. He has no need of our offerings. As St. Chrysostom says, God's love is like the sun, which always gives to the earth. It lights and warms the earth, but we give nothing in return to the sun. The sun has no need of us, but we need the sun. God has no need of us, but we need God. And so God, being moved by a boundless love for us, continuously sends His blessings to us. The greatest testimony of His love for us is that He sent His only-begotten Son into the world – our Lord Jesus Christ, who was sacrificed for us.

Next, the priest says: "And the communion of the holy Spirit be with you all." *The communion of the Holy Spirit* means that after Christ was sacrificed on the cross and we received forgiveness of sins, the grace of the Holy Spirit also began flowing like a crystal-clear river into the Church, watering the vineyard of God so it would produce fruit on its spiritual vines. Faithful Christians sense the Holy Spirit, because He informs them that they are children of God. In the hearts of believers illumined by the Holy Spirit, a secret voice is heard: "God loves you."

In simple words, dear friends, this is the meaning of the Apostolic blessing, heard at every Divine Liturgy. Words inspired by God. These words also proclaim the dogma of the Holy Trinity — Father, Son and Holy Spirit — the three Persons of the Deity Who work together for the world's salvation. Whatever the Father wishes, the Son and the Holy Spirit also wish. "One power, one manifestation, one veneration of the Holy Trinity."

Therefore, glory, honor and worship belong to the Father, the Son and the Holy Spirit.

O Blessed Trinity, have mercy on the world and on us sinners. And you, Apostle Paul, bless us with your apostolic blessing: "The grace of our Lord Jesus Christ and the love of God the Father and the communion of the Holy Spirit be with you all."

"AND WITH THY SPIRIT"

"The grace of our Lord Jesus Christ, and the love of God the Father, and the communion of the Holy Spirit be with you all." This, we said, is the beautiful Apostolic Blessing. It was first said by the chief of the Apostles, Paul. Since then, countless priests and bishops have repeated this blessing, and we briefly explained the meaning of 'grace of Christ,' 'love of the Father,' and 'communion of the Holy Spirit.'

In addition to what we said before, let us note, as theologians observe, that the grace of Christ, the love of God and Father, and the communion of the Holy Spirit are not personal characteristics (such as the Father is unborn, the Son is born, and the Holy Spirit proceeds), but are natural and essential qualifications of God. That is, grace is not only of our Lord Jesus Christ, but is also of the Father and the Holy Spirit; love is not only the Father's, but of Jesus Christ and the Holy Spirit as well; and communion is not only of the Holy Spirit, but of the Father and Son. One God in three Persons, Father, Son and Holy Spirit.

O Holy Trinity, have mercy on the world and on us. Jehovah's Witnesses do not believe in the Holy Trinity; but Holy Scripture itself (which they ever hold in their hands) testifies about the Trinity. The fact that the human mind cannot comprehend this great mystery is not a reason to reject it, for as we have said, mystery is everywhere. Alas, if we establish that 'I accept only what

I understand,' then we would not only reject the existence of the unseen world, but most of the visible one as well. The visible world has its mysteries, too. Let man, then, solve the smaller mysteries before attempting to solve the greater and more difficult ones.

The celebrant priest wishes people grace, love and communion of the Triune God to guide these Christians throughout their lives, but especially now when the Mystery of Holy Eucharist is about to be offered. Hearts should not be dry and barren, but should overflow with the priceless spiritual gifts which come from the source of every gift, the Blessed Trinity.

People, hearing this beautiful apostolic prayer, responding to the priest, say: "And with thy spirit," namely, "The blessing you wished us, we also wish you." If this grace should exist in the hearts of the faithful, so much the more should it be in the heart of the celebrating priest. Shame on that priest who is spiritually empty, yet audaciously approaches the sanctuary wishing others what he himself does not have! But even with such a priest, grace is not hampered from flowing through to water and refresh our souls. The priest is the instrument. May he participate not only with his chanting, but with his soul, for this can be noticed in the way he recites the petitions and prayers!

Grace for God's people, grace for the priest, grace for the entire Body of the Church, which consists of lay people and clergy! You see, spiritual gifts are plentiful!

"And with thy spirit." Here, the soul is called 'spirit.' The soul is immaterial, an imperishable essence existing in everybody. Holy Scripture, too, calls the soul a 'spirit.' When a soul believes in Christ, it receives the grace of the Holy Spirit; it is ennobled, enriched and elevated to higher spiritual levels where the fleshly, carnal and natural man becomes spiritual, as St. Paul teaches (I Corinthians 2:14-16).

St. Athanasios also speaks about the soul's spiritual progress. "Through the undivided Trinity, all souls are born again, and by Him they are purified to shine in mystical glory." According to the teaching of our Church, the life of the body is the soul, and life of the soul is the grace of the Holy Spirit.

Those attending church should be full of spirit, most of all the priest, who is celebrating the Divine Liturgy, and especially at those awesome moments when the great Mystery is offered. No wickedness, vice or passion should dominate, but the Spirit must rule. Thus, what the Church chants should become real: "While we stand in the temple of Thy glory, we stand in heaven." In other words, in church, our bodies touch the earth, but our souls become spirits and are in heaven; spirit, like the angels and archangels, which the Psalm calls a "flame of fire:" "who maketh His angels spirits, and His ministers a flame of fire" (Psalm 103:4).

"And with thy spirit." To what heights God calls us! Clergy and laity must become spirits. Are we? Let's all examine our consciences, and it will answer what state our souls are in.

If we open the Old Testament to the first book, Genesis, chapter 6, and read it carefully, fear and awe will take us, because we also live in a time not too different from that described in Scripture.

It says that many centuries after the creation, people multiplied. They committed crimes and injustices, prostitution and adultery, moving ever further away from God. And what was worse, if someone appeared to counsel them or call them to repentance, they did not believe and mocked him. They lived with no sense of God, worse than beasts. Scripture says that God's Spirit did not exist in these people because they were totally carnal. These carnal 'bodies' had eyes, ears, hands and legs, brain and heart, but all of them served only wickedness. People became cunning like foxes, blood-thirsty like wolves, rapacious like birds of prey, filthy like pigs, debauched like he-goats, vindictive like camels – flesh and only flesh!

What was the result? Heavenly torrents opened and it rained for forty days and nights. Rivers and lakes overflowed and water reached up to the mountain-tops, killing all the animals and people. Only eight individuals, Noah and his family, were spared. A terrible destruction!

These things happened then, but our Lord warned us that a time will come which will be like the times of Noah. We ask, have we reached these terrible days?

How the "And with thy spirit" should teach and reprove us! May we, with earnest repentance, become spirits from flesh, that our souls may one day be worthy to rest "with the spirits of the righteous made perfect."

EAGLES...

Dear friends, in the army there is order, and order is maintained because soldiers carry out the commands of their officers. Are the soldiers lined up? As soon as the officer cries "Attention!" the soldiers stand at attention.

The sight of soldiers carrying out their orders is beautiful. But if the appearance of the soldiers is beautiful as they carry out the commands of their officers, it is incomparably more beautiful to view the congregants present at certain points of the Divine Liturgy when the priest addresses the command: "Let us attend," "Let us stand aright; let us stand in awe," "Wisdom! Let us arise."

Christians attending Church services are like soldiers of a spiritual army, consisting not only of people, but of angels who are lined up around the throne of the supreme God. Those in church should pay attention, so that when the priest gives the order, it is carried out at once. What would you say if a soldier listens to the command "Attention!", and instead of obeying it, he is indifferent?

Christians, soldiers of our Lord Jesus Christ, when you hear the sacred commands, concentrate all your attention, press and force yourselves, so you may do whatever the priest commands. It is impious to ignore these sacred orders, to remain seated on chairs or in a stall when the Church gives the order "Let us arise," asking Christians to stand in body and soul before divine Majesty.

We have heard that in churches in America, when the time comes for the congregation to rise, the priest turns on an electric light, and at once they stand up; but I don't think it is necessary to make the people stand in a mechanical way. The sacred commands are so clear that no other prompting is needed. We must be careful not to let the Divine Liturgy become a series of automatic bodily movements void of meaning or understanding. The Christian should not simply rise from his seat, but his heart should overflow with a deep feeling of reverence.

One of these sacred commands is: "Let us lift up our hearts." Immediately after the apostolic blessing, the priest addresses the people from the Beautiful Gate, lifting up his hands and eyes towards heaven, externally expressing what the sacred order commands – to lift up our hearts. But what does this command mean?

All of us know, the heart is the most important organ for human life. Is the heart in bad condition? The person is in danger of dying from one moment to the next. He is trembling lest his heart suddenly stop functioning. The heart, as an instrument of the body, is like a pump, working day and night, carrying enough blood through veins and arteries annually to fill a reservoir.

The heart is an admirable organ, which alone is enough to prove that God exists. It is true that science is working to create an artificial heart. But science itself is forced to confess that an artificial heart will never reach the state of perfection of a real human heart. God "made everything in wisdom" (Psalm 103:26).

When we hear the word "heart" in the Divine Liturgy, however, we should perceive something superior. Here, heart means all one's internal world. This world is vast and unseen. "Heart" is our thoughts, sentiments, will, *our whole internal world.*

"Let us lift up our hearts." That is to say, the moment the great Mystery of the Holy Eucharist is about to be offered, our minds should think of nothing else but this great Mystery. It is a joy and pleasure to raise our thoughts toward God, as the Prophet David says: "May my words be sweet unto Him, and I will rejoice in the Lord" (Psalm 103:36). Love, this deep feeling, should be directed toward the Person of the God-Man Redeemer, Who comes to be sacrificed for the salvation of the world. Our internal world, overflowing with love, should say, "I will love Thee, O Lord, my strength; the Lord is my foundation and my refuge and my deliverer" (Psalm 17:1). Our will should be subject to the Divine Will and we should conscientiously repeat: "Thy will be done" and: "Not as I will, but as Thou wilt, Father" (Matt. 26:42, 39).

Dear friends, to what heights this command of the Church invites us! It calls us to heavenly heights. As St. Chrysostom says, our souls must leave worldly cares and fly high, becoming eagles. And as the eagle always flies high with its face toward the sun, bathed in the light and traversing the heavens, so too should our souls, with lofty thoughts, gentle feelings, holy sentiments and sacred wishes, attain great, strong spiritual wings like the eagles,' and fly to where Christ is, where His holy Sanctuary is.

Christ Himself said: "Wherever there is a dead body the vultures will gather" (Matt. 24:28). Dead body – in a good sense – is Christ's Body. The souls of pious

Christians are eagles gathering around the precious Body of Christ. Other souls which do not think of Christ or love Him are those dirty birds, ravens, which fly low, searching for something rotten to eat.

"Let us lift up our hearts," says the priest, and the people, hearing this sacred command, answer through the cantor: "We lift them up unto the Lord." That is to say, the congregation affirms that they heard this command, and at this moment their minds are thinking of nothing else, their hearts love nothing else, their wills wish nothing else but Christ. Eagles, flying high, look toward the sun, bathe in the light, and appear brightly in the sky, elevated in the heavenly spheres; and the priest, hearing the affirmation that all are fixed on Christ and are ready to observe the celebration of the Mystery, gives another command: "Let us give thanks unto the Lord."

Before we close this brief homily, let us ask each one: Are we carrying out the command: "Let us lift up our hearts"? Where are our hearts during the Divine Liturgy? Are they with Christ? If so, we are fortunate. But if not, if we think of sinful things, then by saying: "We lift them up unto the Lord," we are caught in a lie! When? During a most sacred moment!

O Lord, have mercy on us and save us.

THE HOLY PENTECOST

VI

THE CONSECRATION OF
THE PRECIOUS GIFTS

BENEFITS SEEN AND UNSEEN

"We give thanks to Thee . . . "

We are at a sacred point in the Divine Liturgy; the moment is approaching when the precious gifts will be consecrated. Our Lord Jesus Christ, before His Last Supper, thanked his heavenly Father because the great moment had arrived when He would offer Himself for the salvation of the world; and the priest, who has come to this point in the Liturgy, when the Mystery of Holy Eucharist will be offered, stands with great reverence before the Holy Table and says the prayer of Consecration over the Precious Gifts.

This prayer begins with: "It is meet and right to hymn Thee, to bless Thee . . . ," and ends with the Exclamation: "And the mercies of the Great God and our Savior Jesus Christ shall be with you all."

Because the Eucharistic Prayer is interrupted at certain points for Exclamations, offering incense, and the hymn "It is very meet to bless Thee, Theotokos," we could divide this very important prayer into four parts: 1. The Eucharistic prayer with the Triumphal Hymn, 2. The Commemoration of the Last Supper, 3. The Invocation of the Holy Spirit to consecrate the Precious Gifts, and 4. The Commemoration of the living and the dead.

We will speak here about the first part of the prayer, which is the following:

"It is meet and right to hymn Thee, to bless Thee, to praise Thee, to give thanks unto Thee, and to worship Thee in every place of Thy dominion: for Thou art God ineffable, inconceivable, invisible, incomprehensible, ever-existing, unchangeable. Out of nothing hast Thou brought us into being, and when we had fallen away, Thou didst raise us up again and Thou hast not ceased to do all things until Thou hadst brought us back up to heaven, and bestowed upon us Thy kingdom which is to come. For all these things, we give thanks unto Thee, and to Thine only-begotten Son, and to Thy Holy Spirit, for all the things of which we know, and for all the benefits both manifest and unseen, which have been bestowed upon us, and we give thanks unto Thee also for this ministry, which Thou dost vouchsafe to receive at our hands, even though there stand beside Thee thousands of Archangels and ten thousands of Angels, the Cherubim and the Seraphim, six-winged, many-eyed, soaring aloft, borne on their wings...."

In this part of the prayer, the priest offers the Triune God thanks and praise. Whoever hears this superb prayer from the lips of a pious priest is led to think about all creation, things animate and inanimate, each one in its own way glorifying and praising the all-powerful, wise and benevolent Creator of the world. There was a time when there was no creation, living or lifeless, neither a visible nor an invisible world. There was neither land nor sea; the earth did not exist. There was no sun, neither was there moon or stars; no men, angels or archangels. Only God existed. Whose mind can conceive of God? What language can describe His majesty? God is inexpressible, that is, we cannot describe Him; He is incomprehensible, we cannot understand His ways. Father,

Son and Holy Spirit, this Triune God, created the world and us from nothing.

When mankind left God's path, fell away and was lost, we were in danger of perishing; but God did not abandon us – He made every effort to save the work of His hands.

By Christ's incarnation, by the power of divine grace, God took fallen mankind and raised it up to heaven, giving us the kingdom of the age to come.

For all these benefits, we thank You, O Holy Trinity. We thank You for Your benevolent acts, some of which are known and others unknown. We thank You also for the Divine Liturgy, which enables us to offer You praise today, although You have no need of our hymns. Thousands of archangels and myriads of angels, the Cherubim and Seraphim surround Your throne and chant the triumphant hymn, "Holy, Holy, Holy Lord of Hosts" (Isaiah 6:3).

The whole of this part of our prayer is excellent, but let us pay special attention to where it calls us to thank God for his works, known and unknown. What are these "known and unknown" benefits? "Known" benefits are those we see and feel. They are our bread, fruits, water, trees, the rays of the sun, the air we breathe – every beat of our hearts is a benevolent act of God! There is no time, not one second when God is not doing us a favor. As a fish lives and moves in water and cannot live outside it, so we live and move in the endless sea of God's benevolent acts.

We swim in the ocean of God's benefits. If Divine Providence were to stop providing its support for just one moment, we could not live. We live because God loves us and opens His omnipotent hand, spreading his immeasureable bounty from East to West, over the whole earth.

But other than God's "known" benefits, there are also His "unknown" acts. These are the ones we cannot perceive. Only one who believes in God is able to perceive these benefits, for the believer can see much more than the unbeliever. The believer knows that behind every event, no matter how unpleasant, God's love is hidden, a love that even offers us a bitter cup, not to make us perish, but to save us. It is offered as a doctor offers bitter medicines to his patients. Yes, God is behind everything!

So many unpleasant things that have taken place in the course of events, making us feel pain or cry, were really God's benevolent acts! Being short-sighted, we cannot see that behind dark clouds there is a silver lining, that the sun is shining. When the world closes one door, God opens another one, for "in all things God works for good with those who love him" (Rom. 8:28).

O God, we thank You from the bottoms of our hearts. We thank You for all Your good acts, known and unknown.

THE TRIUMPHANT HYMN

In our last homily, we looked at the first part of the Prayer of Consecration, which the priest reads at the Holy Altar. His heart overflows in gratitude to the Triune God for His countless blessings. His tongue cannot find words to express this gratitutde. Imperfect and small as we are, because of our sinfulness, we crawl around like worms on the face of the earth, but dare to raise our faces toward the infinite God!

The angels are more perfect than we are. They see divine things more clearly. They are our friends and helpers when we do good works. When they see us in our sacred endeavor to reach the summit of divine things, they come and join their angelic voices with ours. Angels and archangels were once heard singing the Triumphant Hymn; but now, during the Divine Liturgy, we hear instead the hearty voices of the cantors.

The Triumphant Hymn is "Holy, Holy, Holy Lord of Hosts, heaven and earth are full of Thy glory, Hosanna in the Highest; blessed is he that cometh in the Name of the Lord. Hosanna in the Highest."

First of all, let's see what "triumphant" means. A "triumphant" hymn is one that soldiers sing after a victorious battle. Those of our readers who are older and took part in battles which glorified Greece, remember when soldiers, who with the help of God and His most pure Mother, climbed the steep summits where only eagles flew, and there raised the Greek flag, began singing patriotic songs, full of enthusiasm and joy, proclaiming victory and triumph.

Aside from these battles and victories, however, there is another infinitely superior one. It is the fight, the spiritual fight, which Christ fought against the devil, a battle which took place on Golgotha and ended with the victory and triumph of the Crucified Lord. Satan, the age-old enemy, was defeated, and ever since, everyone who believes and looks on the Cross conquers and triumphs. The angels are the spectators of this spiritual struggle. Seeing our victory and the triumph of the Cross, they rejoice and sing the Triumphant Hymn: "Holy, Holy, Holy Lord of Sabaoth...."

The Triumphant Hymn is a combination of two hymns. The one is the angelic hymn mentioned by the prophet Isaiah (6:3), and the other is the one which the people of Jerusalem chanted when they received Christ as victor in their city (Matt. 21:9).

If we open the Book of Isaiah, we will see that the sixth chapter describes a vision. The Prophet saw the house of God and the glory which covered it. He saw a high throne, not like one of earthly kings, but one suspended in the air, and around this throne he saw angels. The angels were so amazed at the divine majesty that they covered their faces and their legs with their wings, and with two other wings they flew, chanting "Holy, Holy, Holy Lord of Sabaoth; the whole earth is full of His glory." The intensity of their voices was so great that the door of the temple opened and it filled with the smoke of incense; and the Prophet, seeing this astonishing spectacle, trembled. He felt his sinfulness and insignificance, and he said: "Woe is me, for I am pricked to the heart; for being a man, and having unclean lips, I dwell in the midst of a people having unclean lips; and I have seen with mine eyes the King, the Lord of Hosts!" That is to say, "What a wretched man I am! This very moment I feel my sinfulness. What am I? – an unclean man with an impure mouth, living with a people who are unclean and have impure mouths. But in spite of this, today I saw the King with my own eyes, the Lord of Hosts."

This is the vision that the Prophet Isaiah saw. This vision is revealing. It praises the grandeur of God, it preaches that the Lord of Sabaoth is One, that is, that He is the Lord of Hosts who rules heaven and earth, the Lord of angels and men. All the earth glows from His glory. Even the smallest things, if we examine them carefully, have their mysteries, dimly revealing the Lord of Sabaoth, the Lord in three Persons, Father, Son and Holy Spirit, who cooperate harmoniously for the good of creation, to preserve the natural and spiritual world. It is for this reason the word "Holy" (which in an absolute sense is proper only to God) is repeated three times in the angelic hymn. The Father is holy, the Son is holy, the Holy Spirit is holy. O Holy Trinity, glory to Thee!

We are not left out of hymning and praising God. Uniting our voices with those of the angels, we say, "Hosanna in the Highest; blessed is he that cometh in the name of the Lord. Hosanna in the Highest."

This hymn is taken from the Book of Psalms. In the 117th Psalm, a glorious day is prophesied, when people will magnificently welcome Christ, the victorious and triumphant one, saying: "This is the day which the Lord hath made; let us rejoice and be glad therein. O Lord, save now; O Lord, send now prosperity. Blessed is he that cometh in the name of the Lord" (vs. 24-26). Really glorious was the day when Christ entered Jerusalem, before He was sacrificed on the Cross. Thousands of people, gathering in Jerusalem to celebrate the Jewish passover, hearing that Christ was coming, went out of the city and greeted Him with unprecedented expressions of joy and enthusiasm. The entire city shook with cheers. They held branches in their hands and shook them. They spread their clothes on the streets as the King of Israel passed, and they all cried aloud: "Hosanna," which means: "O Lord, save, You are our Redeemer."

So, dear friends, if the time for greeting Christ was one of great commotion and enthusiasm for the Hebrews who greeted Him, how much more should it be a time of enthusiasm and admiration for us at the Divine Liturgy when the bloodless sacrifice is about to be offered? Let us hold a feeling of gratitude – not a temporary one, like the Hebrews, who one day shouted: "Hosanna," and a few days later shouted: "Crucify Him!" (Mark 15:13-14).

THAT NIGHT...

As we all know, dear readers, our Lord Jesus Christ performed miracles during His earthly ministry. He changed water into wine; he walked on the sea; He stopped the wind which raised great waves; He fed thousands of hungry people with a few loaves of bread; He gave sight to the blind; He opened the ears of the deaf; He made the dumb speak; He made paralytics get up from their beds and walk; He healed lepers and others who suffered with incurable illnesses; He raised the dead, like Lazarus, going to his grave after four days and bringing him back to life.

Christ performed so many miracles that the Evangelist John said, if someone were to sit down and record all of them, there would be so many books that there would not be enough space to contain them all. So many books would be needed to give a detailed account of the miracles Christ performed and continues to perform — the rays of the sun might be counted, but Christ's miracles could never be numbered.

All of Christ's miracles are instructive in nature. All of them together and each separately, when examined carefully, show that Christ is God, that He is the Second Person of the Holy Trinity, the only-begotten Son of God, Whom the heavenly Father by His infinite love sent into the world, so that whoever believes in Him will not be lost, but will have eternal life.

As the Divine Liturgy moves on to its climax, the priest invites us not to remember any of Christ's miracles, but to call to mind His Cross and noble Passion, endured for our sake – to remember the sacrifice offered on Golgotha.

Why is this? Why such emphasis on His sacrifice and not on His miracles? This question was asked by one holy commentator on the Divine Liturgy, Nicholas Kavasilas. He answers his own question, saying that the suffering which Christ endured "produced our salvation, but His miracles only demonstrated our salvation." In plain language, what the commentator wants to say is, that no matter how many miracles Christ performed, if he did not sacrifice Himself on the cross, we would not have been saved. It is impossible for us to be saved, to be raised up into a spiritual life without the sacrifice, the Blood of the God-man, and for this reason, we are called to remember His salutary Passion.

The Divine Liturgy is a *remembrance of the sacrifice* that Christ offered.

Every hour of our earthly life has great meaning. Among these hours, however, there are some which evoke special feelings for the faithful. Such are the hours our Lord spent on the last night of His earthly life – from sunset on Great Thursday until dawn on Great Friday.

That night reminds us of the hours Christ spent in the Garden of Gethsemane, His anxious prayer, sweat falling from His face like drops of blood, kneeling under the moon's pale light, saying: "My Father, if it is possible, take this cup away from me! But not what I want, but what you want. . . Your will be done (Matt. 26:39-42).

We are reminded of his three beloved disciples sleeping on the grass while Christ was in agony. We are reminded of the sounds which the soldiers' weapons made as they came to arrest Christ, being led by the disciple, Judas. We are reminded of the reply Christ gave to the soldiers, and of when Christ, arrested, was bound and brought to trial at the house of Annas and Caiaphas. Finally, we are reminded of Great Friday morning, when Christ was brought before Pontius Pilate.

O holy night! Night of the Passion and sacrifice of Christ – you remind us of all this! The Divine Liturgy also reminds us of all these events, especially in the inspired Prayer of Consecration. And it reminds us, along with all the rest, of the Last Supper when Christ dined with his disciples, the Mystical Supper which also took place that night.

What happened at that Supper? If we open the Gospels and read those chapters, we will see what happened. Our Lord Jesus Christ, approaching the last days of his life, expressed his desire to eat his last Passover with His disciples. But where? He did not own a house – He was born in a cave! The dinner was therefore prepared in the house of one of His friends.

It was the eve of the great feast of the Passover, according to the Hebrew calendar. Before the dinner, however, Christ overheard His disciples arguing. They were quarreling about who would be first in the new kingdom which Christ was to establish. Christ felt sad. He was going to His sacrifice, to the most cruel death man ever suffered, and His disciples were arguing about rank. But Christ gave them the needed lesson. He put on a servant's apron, filled a basin with water, and washed the feet of all His disciples, even those of Judas. He so taught the disciples that whoever serves others more will hold the most important place in His kingdom.

Christ wanted His disciples to be servants and not exploiters of the world.

After that, they sat down to supper. Christ blessed the food. He took bread in His holy hands, broke it and gave His disciples some of it, saying: "Take, eat; this is my body" (Matt. 26:26). Then He took wine and invited His disciples to drink saying: "Drink ye all of it, for this is my blood, of the new testament, which is shed for many for the remission of sins" (Matt. 26:26-28). And He commanded them, that what he had just done, they must also do themselves, with all the faithful throughout the centuries: "Do this in remembrance of me" (Luke 26:19).

The priest reads the second part of the Prayer of Consecration with pious feeling. Among other things, he says: "And He, when He had come, fulfilling all the dispensation appointed for us, on the night in which He was betrayed, or rather, gave Himself up for the life of the world, took bread. . . ."

O holy night, on which the Mystical Supper took place! From that night on, the Church has never forgotten the Lord's command to offer the Mystical Supper, to invite Christians to approach the Holy Table and receive Holy Communion, the Body and Blood of Christ.

THE MIRACLE

"Thy Gifts of what is Thine, do we offer to Thee,
in all we do and for all Thy blessings...."

People are always looking for miracles, but miracles can be found everywhere. That is, there are things which, in spite of all our wisdom and science, we cannot do. Wherever we turn our eyes, whether we look at the earth or toward heaven, we see wonders. Not only the countless stars, the huge celestial planets which whirl through the boundless universe, but even the tiniest particles into which our creation can be divided, the atoms, are all created in such perfection, in such wisdom, that they cause us to wonder.

One question is asked by every thinking person — Who made all these natural phenomena? The answer: they were all created by God's word, as Holy Scripture says: "For He spoke, and they were made" (Psalm 32:9). God said: "Let there be light" and there was light (Gen. 1:3). One thing came into existence and then another, and they continue to exist by natural laws which the creator has established. In regard to mankind, Holy Scripture says that God's interest was special. "According to the image of God He made man, male and female He made them" (Gen. 1:27-28).

The words "increase and multiply," St. Chrysostom observes, became natural law, *creative law*, and with the union of the two sexes, we became creators of other human beings, other people, and as we multiplied more and more, the population of the earth reached billions.

If God had not said "increase and multiply," if He had not planted creative, reproductive power in us, the birth of other people would have been impossible. But God's words "increase and multiply" had such creative power that it lasts up to our own times. In the same way, Christ's words, uttered on the first Great Thursday when He created the Mystery of Holy Eucharist, have creative power: "Take ye, eat; this is my Body . . . ," "Drink of it ye all; this is my Blood. . . ."

When the priest stands before the Holy Table, repeats these creative words of Christ and invokes the Holy Spirit, a miracle takes place. The bread becomes the Body of Christ and the wine becomes the Blood of Christ. This miracle gives us Christ as He was born of the Virgin Mary and crucified for us. Although it does not appear to our natural eyes, it is understood by faith. This miracle bloodlessly continues the sacrifice of the Cross.

Roman Catholics say that the priest's words: "Take ye, eat . . . ," and "Drink ye all . . . ," are enough to make this miracle take place; but our Church, according to the teaching of the Fathers, considers these words to be the condition of the miracle, but for it to be carried out, it is necessary to invoke the Holy Spirit at every Divine Liturgy, as is done in the other sacraments.

St. Chrysostom relates the example of the prophet Elijah. To prove to idolaters that the God he worshipped was the true God, the prophet invited these people to the top of Mt. Carmel. There, a makeshift altar was erected and the pagan priests sacrificed their calf and said prayers to their false gods, asking them to send fire for their sacrifice. But in spite of their prayers, which lasted hours, the fire did not come. But when the prophet Elijah took his calf and placed it on the altar, the people stood watching and waiting to see what would happen. The prophet said a short prayer to God, asking Him to send fire down upon the slaughtered animal, so that the sacrifice could take place. Immediately, fire fell from heaven and the slaughtered animal was burned. The fire was so hot that even the stones burned. The people that saw this miracle believed in God, saying that the God in whom the prophet Elijah believed was the true God (III Kings 17:22-40).

This miracle is small in comparison to the one which the priest performs at every celebration of the Divine Liturgy. He asks not for fire like that which came down upon the altar of Elijah, but for the Holy Spirit, so that the sacrifice may be performed to illumine our hearts with the light of grace from the Holy Spirit.

Before the priest invokes the Holy Spirit, he says at the end of his silent prayer: "Thy Gifts, of what is Thine, do we offer to Thee, in all we do and for all Thy blessings." That is to say, whatever we offer for sacrifice is not ours, O Lord. The bread and wine come from You. You are the source of all blessings. You are our Creator and Benefactor. We thank You from the bottoms of our hearts for all Your blessings. We thank You at this sacred moment, when the greatest of miracles is about to be offered.

Then with a loud voice, the priest, moved by pious feelings and fear of God, prays that the Holy Spirit come, so that the bread may become the Body of Christ and the wine, the Blood of Christ. These are the words of Invocation:

"And make this bread the precious Body of Thy Christ. Amen. And that which is in the Cup, the Precious Blood of Thy Christ. Amen. Changing them by Thy Holy Spirit. Amen. Amen. Amen."

This is the most sacred moment of the Divine Liturgy. The priest kneels before the Holy Table and the people in attendance should also kneel and pray silently while the cantors chant: "We praise Thee, we bless Thee, we give thanks unto Thee, O Lord, and we entreat Thee, O our God."

In the Slavic Church of times past, there was a custom that when this sacred moment came, to ring the church bells joyously to announce to the world that a miracle was taking place. I ordered that in our diocese, during this holy minute, the church bells should be rung so that even those who did not attend church would know that a miracle incomparably great is taking place in the Orthodox church.

THE BENEFITS OF THE MYSTERY

My dear readers, we said in our last homily that the holiest moment of the Divine Liturgy is when the priest invokes the Holy Spirit to come and change the bread and wine into the Body and Blood of our Lord Jesus Christ. The part of the Divine Liturgy which contains the Invocation and Consecration is composed of 109 Greek words, which all have their own special meaning, words which, according to one interpretor of the Liturgy, Father Gervasios Paraskevopoulos, are hallowed by the centuries. These words, repeated continuously everywhere, are worthy of wonder. They used to bring tears to the eyes of emperors and slaves, patriarchs and monks. They were heard in the church of Hagia Sophia and in the desert caves. They have the power to cause miracles in our souls.

After the final Invocation ("changing them by the Holy Spirit"), the deacon says: "Amen, Amen, Amen." This Amen at the end of the Invocation is a fervent prayer. It serves to make the priest's request become a reality, whether or not he is morally worthy to celebrate the Holy Eucharist. This great miracle takes place even at the hands of the most unworthy priest, provided he be canonically ordained.

After the "Amen," the priest continues, saying:

"So that they may be to those that receive them for the purification of the soul, for the remission of sins, for the fellowship of Thy Holy Spirit, and for boldness to approach Thee, neither unto judgement not unto condemnation. Again we offer unto Thee this reasonable Service for those who have fallen asleep in the Faith: Fathers, Forefathers, Patriarchs, Prophets, Apostles, Preachers, Evangelists, Martyrs, Confessors, Ascetics, and every righteous spirit in faith made perfect."

This prayer mentions, first of all, those for whom the Divine Liturgy is offered. The purpose of this, as we said, is the *Anamnesis* (remembrance) of the Lord's holy Passion, but also the *Communion* of Christ's Body and Blood by all the faithful, and, through Holy Communion, *blessing.*

The benefits which come from Holy Communion are priceless. The priest prays that Holy Communion will, first of all, purify the soul. What is "purification of soul?" The impure soul is the worldly person, not moved by the grandeur of God, not attentive. When the Divine Liturgy is offered, when miracles occur, the worldly person, unillumined by God's Spirit, does not pay attention – he is indifferent, sleeping. Even if the heavens were full of thunder and lightning and the earth shook, he would sleep. This is a very dangerous situation for the soul to be in. Spiritual sleep is deadly. We must awaken ourselves from this deadly sleep; and when we wake up, we will begin to pay attention, and none of God's wonders will leave us unmoved. O Christ, give us attention to holy things, so that our souls, ever awake, will not fall into satan's traps. Make us ever attentive to Your command: "Watch and pray, that ye enter not into temptation" (Matt. 26.41).

Holy Communion also gives us other priceless blessings. One of them is forgiveness of sins. Sin is forgiven through Holy Communion.

"How?" some will ask. I know that sins are forgiven in the Mystery of Repentance and Confession. I sin; I recognize my sinfulness; I cry and feel sorry, go to my spiritual Father, confess my sins, and the Father Confessor declares my forgiveness.

You now say that Holy Communion forgives sins? We answer this question as follows: Forgiveness of sins derives its power from Christ's sacrifice on the Cross. If Christ were never sacrificed, if He had not shed His precious Blood, there would be no forgiveness. Jesus' Blood cleanses us from every sin (I John 1:7). Forgiveness of sins depends on this sacrifice. Forgiveness is certainly given in the Mystery of Confession, but it is confirmed in the Mystery of Holy Eucharist. Remember the parable of the Prodigal Son? The father, immediately after the return of his prodigal son, forgave him, sealing the fact that he forgave him by sacrificing the prize calf, offering it in celebration (Luke 15:2-3).

These two Sacraments, therefore, are connected to one another and get their power from the inexhaustible fountain of grace which flows from the Cross. "I forgive you," says Christ in the Mystery of Confession; "I forgive you, and to confirm this, I offer the prize calf on my table!" Participating in the Divine Eucharist is a demonstration of God's love for us when we sincerely repent.

Purification of soul is one spiritual benefit of Holy Communion; forgiveness of sins is another. There is a third and a fourth benefit. When we receive Holy Communion, we are united with Christ. We receive Divine grace, which helps us in our fight against sin. Through Holy Communion, our hearts, being like unclean stables, become God's mansions, palaces of heaven, residing places of the Holy Spirit. The Holy Spirit illumines, brightens and beautifies our souls.

Holy Communion is also "for the fulfillment of the Kingdom of Heaven." That is to say, with Holy Communion, the seeds of eternal life are planted in us and continuously develop, finding fulfillment, complete development in the Kingdom of Heaven. With Holy Communion, we gain the Kingdom of Heaven, Paradise. For this reason, Holy Communion is called the "medicine of immortality, the antidote for death." It is a medicine which overcomes death and bestows eternal life.

Great are the benefits of Holy Communion. But when? When the Christian partakes *worthily*. When we approach Holy Communion without faith, without sincere repentance, tears, or the decision to fight sin (for which the God-Man went to the Cross), then Holy Communion is not for our spiritual benefit, but becomes the cause of our condemnation. Holy communion is a fire which burns those who partake of it unworthily.

Uniting our prayer with that of the priest, we should pray to God that Holy Communion does not become "judgement" or "condemnation" for us.

COMMEMORATIONS

On Golgotha, a unique sacrifice was offered, the sacrifice of our Lord Jesus Christ. This sacrifice is of incalculable value. Sinners vainly tried to obtain forgiveness of their sins. No matter how many sacrifices they offered, it was impossible to get redemption, because sin has such a weight of guilt that neither men nor angels can lift it. The sacrifices offered by all the people of the ancient world, even those of the Hebrews themselves, were not only proof of their sinfulness and guilt, but the representation in shadows and "types" of the unique sacrifice which was to be offered for the world's life and salvation.

As we have often said, Christ is the one who lifted the weight of the world's sin up on His Cross, liberating the human race from guilt and its cruel slavery to sin. Whatever people say or write about the sacrifice on Golgotha, they will never finish the subject: it is a great mystery. Even intellectuals will never understand this mystery, that Christ suffered "instead of us" and "for us." Only the one who is aware of his sinfulness, and approaches the crucified Redeemer of the world with faith, kneeling to venerate Christ's immaculate Passion, asking forgiveness of sins, only this person can in some measure understand the importance of Christ's sacrifice on the Cross.

Forgiveness of sins! This lofty gift is given "in the Blood of our Lord Jesus Christ." If we are grateful to those who offer their blood in emergencies to save lives, how much more should we be grateful to Him Whose veins were opened on the Cross. He gave His Blood, pure and precious, to save us from spiritual death?

The Blood of Christ! The drops of this which dripped from His holy hands and feet — how can we talk about it? — became a great and inexhaustible river in which sinners of every age are washed. These drops of Blood, on every creature which suffers and groans from the sin of the first man and woman, have a mysterious and beneficial effect, and have even reached into dark Hades, where billions of souls (living before the time of Christ) were longing for the day of redemption. Yes, the immense power of Christ's redemptive sacrifice reached and still reaches into Hades. Therefore, when the mystical sacrifice of the God-man is offered on the Holy Altar, the priest remembers not only those attending the service, not only those who are scattered in the four corners of the earth fighting the good fight of faith and virtue, but also those who have died and are now in eternity. This is because they, too, are alive; their souls live, awaiting the Day of Judgement, when their bodies will be resurrected to be reunited with their souls. And these souls too, even having reached high states of virtue, have need of the benevolent influence of Christ's sacrifice.

No one is saved without the Blood of Christ. Everyone needs this sacrifice. Christ's sacrifice has universal influence, and as the sun sends its rays to give light and warmth to all creation, so Christ, who shines like the sun in the Holy Sanctuary, sends His benevolent rays to all creation, to the whole Church, to the whole universe.

After the Consecration of the precious gifts, the priest stands before the Holy Table and begins the commemorations, saying:

"... Again we offer unto Thee this reasonable Service for those who have fallen asleep in the Faith, Forefathers, Fathers, Patriarchs, Prophets, Apostles, Preachers, Evangelists, Martyrs, Confessors, Ascetics and every righteous spirit in faith made perfect."

All the names of those who lived their lives in faith and holiness are worthy of remembrance, because the Saints are mankind's benefactors, who by their illuminating teachings and holy examples, taught and spiritually benefited humanity. They were and still are the light and salt of the human race.

All the Saints are worthy of commemoration, but above all others the Blessed Virgin. The holy Theotokos has a special position in the Church. She is placed above the angels and archangels. That is why her name is commemorated by these words:

"Especially for our most holy, pure, blessed, glorified Lady, Theotokos and Ever-Virgin Mary."

And the people answer with the cantors:

"It is very meet to bless Thee, Theotokos, the ever-blessed and most pure and Mother of our God. Thee that art more honorable than the Cherubim and incomparably more glorious than the Seraphim, that, without spot of sin, didst bear God the Logos: Thee, verily the Birth-giver of God, do we magnify."

After this honorary commemoration of the most holy Theotokos, the priest commemorates the name of St. John the Forerunner, who, according to Christ's own words, was the holiest of all the men of the Old Testament. The priest then commemorates the holy, glorious and honored Apostles, the Saints of the particular day, and all those who ended their earthly lives, the ones "who have fallen asleep," as the prayer calls them. For death is not annihilation, but a sleep, so far as the body is concerned, from which it will awaken at the Resurrection of the Dead. The priest then commemorates the names of bishops, priests and monks, and generally, all those who contribute their services to the Church. In addition, he prays for the whole world, for the holy Orthodox Church, for political authorities, for the army, and he prays that peace may prevail in the world, so that we may live in harmony and love.

The priest especially commemorates the name of the bishop of his diocese and asks God to protect him "with safety, honor, health and length of days, to teach aright the word of truth." At this time, the Christians attending the service follow the Church's command, "And of those each one of us has in mind," silently bringing to mind the names of their beloved living and dead. There is great benefit in commemorating and in an ardent Christian prayer.

THE UNITY OF THE FAITH

We have said that Holy Communion is a sun which illuminates, warms and gives life. If we take a mirror and break it into pieces, each piece of the mirror becomes itself a mirror; and so Christ's Body and Blood in the Holy Communion, even the tiniest portions, not only reflect the Lord's glory, but is itself the same Lord, our Lord Jesus Christ. Therefore, great heed must be paid not only by the celebrating priest, but by every believer who comes to receive Holy Communion, so that even the smallest bits of the holy elements do not fall. Christ exists even in the tiniest piece of Holy Communion.

Christ the invisible, became visible at the Incarnation, acquiring human form. He again becomes visible each time the Divine Liturgy is offered in the forms of bread and wine.

Believers come to Christ, Who appears in the Mystery of Holy Eucharist, to offer them mercy, comfort and support, strength to overcome the world, the flesh and the devil, and prepare them to move from Church Militant to Church Triumphant. Holy Communion instills Christ within the human heart. Every believer who receives Holy Communion becomes a *small Christ*. Even souls who have departed from this world in repentance are benefited when their names are commemorated at the Divine Liturgy after the Consecration.

The Church, sweet Mother, loving to all Her children and even to those who grieve her, turns her affectionate face to the whole world, to young and old, living and dead, and prays that God's mercy be poured out in the Blood of Christ. Thus, the Church's prayer before the Holy Altar acquires a universal dimension. The holy Paten, which holds Christ's Body, becomes a symbol of the whole Church, the whole world. It is like the voice of Christ saying: "For God so loved the world, that he gave his only begotten Son, that whosoever believeth in him should not perish, but have everlasting life" (John 3:16).

Christ, the Body and Blood of Christ on the Holy Altar, Who could possibly believe in our all-wise, omnipotent and all-good God, Who created the world out of nothing, and question the validity of Divine Eucharist? Woe to those who dare open their mouths and say that Orthodox Christians do not partake of the Body and Blood of Christ, but bread and wine only? What a sin, what a blasphemy! This is the most horrible blasphemy – blasphemy against the Holy Spirit, which cannot be forgiven.

But if Christ is on the Holy Altar, the Blessed Lord to whom all prayers are addressed, what is the significance of the petition for the precious Gifts, which takes place after the commemoration of the most holy Theotokos, of the Forerunner, of the Saints, of the living and the dead? Why does the priest say: "For these precious Gifts which have been offered and sanctified, let us pray to the Lord?" Is there not a contradiction? In answer, we say that there is no contradiction. An explanation for this petition could be the following:

We do not question the fact that the holy Body and Blood of Christ are on the Altar, but there is concern that some receiving Holy Communion may do so unworthily, and as a result will not receive the grace of the All-Holy

Spirit. There is concern that the pearls may fall before the swine, that is to say, to people who are unrepentant and morally unclean. The Holy Mysteries must be protected from any kind of desecration, be it from people receiving Communion unworthily, or from vandals or invaders, who break into holy places and profane the holy things.

Nine other petitions follow this one, constituting a "golden chain" of prayers. But since we have already explained eight of these petitions, we will not come back to them. We will say only a few words about the last one: "Asking for the unity of the Faith and for the communion of the Holy Spirit, let us commend ourselves and one another and our whole life to Christ our God."

In this last petition, we are asking for the unity of the faith. We can understand what "unity of the Faith" means if we read the farewell of Christ to His disciples on the night of Great ("Holy") Thursday. It is found in chapters 13 through 17 of the Gospel according to St. John. It is so touching that an ancient teacher of the Church was always moved in reading them. His eyes would fill with tears, seeing Christ's infinite love for us. The prayer Christ addressed ten times to his heavenly Father was for the unity of the Faith, that His disciples be united, so that the world would see their love and unity and believe in Him. He prays for them to be as united with each other as He is with His Father. He asks for complete union. His words are: "I pray that they all may be one; as thou, Father, art in me, and I in thee, that they also may be one in us; that the world may believe that thou hast sent me" (John 17:21).

Unity of the faithful is Christ's ardent wish. He wishes that all be in union as though they were one man.

Unfortunately, however, Christians would not keep their unity. Alas! It has been broken. People who did not accept what the Orthodox Church teaches, or who disagreed with the way She is governed, left the Church and created schisms and heresies. And from the old heresies and schisms, new ones were formed, so that today there are thousands of them.

People of the earth! Listen to the prayer of the Church, the prayer of Christ. Put aside your errors, divisions and schisms. Repent and return to the Orthodox Church. Love one another, and then the power of the Christian world will shine. Christians of the world, unite!

THE MULTIPLICATION OF LOAVES

VII

THE LORD'S PRAYER

"OUR FATHER WHO ART IN HEAVEN"

The sacrifice, my beloved brethren, has been offered. The miracle took place: the bread became the body of Christ; the wine became the blood of Christ. The spiritual table is now ready, it awaits those who shall partake from it.

In the ancient Church, the Church of martyrs, all those who attended the Divine Liturgy, except for a few who for various sins were excluded from Holy Communion, approached and partook of it. In fact it was for this reason that the Liturgy took place. It is not only irregular but also disrespectful to the Divine Eucharist for the Divine Liturgy to be celebrated and no one to come forward to receive Holy Communion.

Imagine someone preparing a costly dinner, inviting his friends, his friends coming and none of them wanting to eat the choice foods. How saddened this man would be by the behaviour of his friends? He prepared this table for no reason, then? From this we can understand, beloved, how much disrespect is shown to the Lord by those who, though they participate in the Divine Liturgy and do not have a serious reason for not receiving Holy Communion, do not come forward to receive it.

But before Christians are called to Commune, the priest, who stands before the Holy Table, addresses an ardent petition to the Lord. He prays, that is to say, that the Lord will enable all, clergy and laity, to draw near to the spiritual table, to receive the awesome and heavenly sacrament with a clear conscience, and thus communing worthily to receive forgiveness of sins, the communion of the Holy Spirit and be made worthy of the Kingdom of Heaven. Not for condemnation, but for life eternal for all, should Holy Communion be. Listen to what this beautiful prayer says:

"We entrust to Thee, loving Master, our whole life and hope, and we ask, pray, and entreat: make us worthy to partake of Thy heavenly and awesome Mysteries from this holy and spiritual Table with a clear conscience; for the remission of sins, forgiveness of transgressions, communion of the Holy Spirit, inheritance of the kingdom of heaven, confidence before Thee, and not in judgment of condemnation."

After this prayer the following petition is said audibly: "And make us worthy, O Master, with confidence and without fear of condemnation, to dare call Thee, the heavenly God, Father, and to say." And then all the people together should say clearly and devoutly the Lord's Prayer.

About the Lord's Prayer, past and contemporary theologians have written many books. The Lord's Prayer is an ocean of divine teaching. A small prayer, which is, however, greater than all the prayers ever heard on earth. For the Lord's Prayer is the prayer that Christ Himself said – hence its name – and which He gave as an example for all the believers of all ages.

This prayer starts with the invocation: "Our Father, Who art in heaven." We have heard these words thousands of times. And, unfortunately, because of continuous repetitions, they do not impress us the way they should. There are impious souls who, when they hear some person speaking about God, mock him and say: "Leave him alone with his Ourfather. . . ." We have come to the point where the most beautiful prayer in the world, a prayer which at other times brought tears to the eyes of believers, is today made the subject of mockery.

"Our Father." The ancient world before Christ were in ignorance as regards the true God. The ancient Greeks imagined that gods lived on the peaks of Olympus and from there, filled with wrath and indignation, threw thunderbolts and poisonous arrows here to earth. The Hebrews certainly had a clearer idea about God, but the height of divine teaching had not been revealed to them. God was God only of the Hebrews.

But Christ came and with one word, which we do not come in across in any other religion of the world, He gave us to understand to what heights it raises the meaning of God. And that word is the term "Father." God is Father, and we who believe in God are His children.

"Our Father." What an honor for men! The most humble and despised person, to whom no one pays any attention, according to the invocation of this prayer, becomes a member of a great family whose Father and Leader is God. A certain preacher called "Princes" those poor for whom he used to provide food during the German occupation. Yes, princes not of this world but of heaven, princes of the most high origin. The poorest person can lift up the eyes of his soul and say to God: "My Father." And a mystical voice is heard in the depths of human existence; a voice which brings peace, love and assurance; a voice, which the saints heard and are hearing: "Father! My Father!" (Rom. 8:15). That is to say, my God, I am your child. And since I am Your child, I find consolation in Your fatherly bosom, and have nothing to fear.

But in addition to this we must pay attention to something else in the invocation of this prayer. We must pay attention to the word "our." We do not say "my Father," but "our Father." Christ instructed us to address our prayer using the plural and not the singular number. And this, because during the time of our prayer we must not have in mind only ourselves and our own needs and desires. We are not alone on earth. Near us there is a multitude of people, connected with us not only by the natural but by the supernatural bond, with the bond of faith in Christ. We, all the faithful, belong to the great family called Christianity, and specifically to the Orthodox Eastern Church (or Eastern Orthodox Church). Our Father is God and our Mother is the Church.

"Our Father, Who art in heaven." You, O God, dominate the universe. Your glory is infinite, immeasurable. The heavens give us a small idea of your glory with its countless stars — the heavens which extend so far, where if someone even travels at the speed of light, will need millions of years to cross.

My God! The mind becomes giddy before Your glory. But is this the only heaven that exists? There are other, spiritual heavens. And a person's heart can become one of them. Our heavenly Father! You are so far, where no one can reach you. But You are also so close, where we can touch You and feel You.

"HALLOWED BE THY NAME"

"THY KINGDOM COME"

We continue in the interpretation of the "Lord's Prayer." We said in the preceding homily that we are the children of God. And since we are God's children, we must try to resemble the heavenly Father. And as a child resembles its own father, in the same way Christians should resemble their heavenly Father: they should be distinguished for their virtues, which are the recognizeable characteristics of the heavenly Father.

God is love; and love should make the Christians distinct (from others). Every other virtue, which God has to the absolute degree, should exist to a relative degree in Christians, too. Do those virtues exist in contemporary Christians? Is there love, or truth, or justice? Is there mercy and philanthropy? Alas! These divine virtues, which should distinguish Christians from heretics and unbelievers, are not in most Christians. Hatred, enmity, jealousy and malice reign in them.

Contemporary Christians present themselves not as children of God, but as children of the devil. What a pitiful phenomenon! The Hebrews boasted that they were the children of Abraham. But Christ, Who knew their wickedness and malice, Who knew that they had none of the virtues that the patriarch Abraham had, challenged them and said that they were the sons of another father, namely children of the devil (John 8:44).

Let us uproot, then, from our hearts every evil and let us plant every virtue, and then with courage and boldness we shall address the heavenly Father and say: "Our Father, Who art in heaven." Not cartoon characters, not caricatures, we should be beautiful images of a true Christian life, images of God.

After the invocation, the petitions of the Lord's Prayer start. And these, in order, are the following:

1. Hallowed be Thy name.

2. Thy Kingdom come.

3. Thy will be done on earth as it is in heaven.

4. Give us this day our daily bread.

5. And forgive us our trespasses as we forgive those who trespass against us.

6. And lead us not into temptation.

7. But deliver us from the evil one.

Let us look at the first petition. It is not a request which concerns the satisfaction of a bodily and material needs. In the first petition we are not asking for food, clothing and other material things from God. The first three petitions are spiritual. This way Christ wants to show us that first of all we must ask for the Kingdom of God, and afterwards for material things. The cardinal point of our life must be our faith and love of Christ. Just as in a railroad train the engine goes first and following behind are the cars, in the same way in life faith in God must be first. This must direct, govern and regulate the entire life of Christians. Earth must not swallow heaven, but heaven must lead, inspire and direct the earth. Not matter first, but the spirit.

"Hallowed be Thy name." We ask that God's name be hallowed. Why? Is not God's name holy? Certainly it is holy in itself, that is to say independently of whether people venerate it or not. All of the blasphemies of the world cannot minimize the glory of God's name in the least, just as all of the spitting of people cannot put out the sun, much less reach it.

When we say "Hallowed be Thy name," we mean that we Christians must live with such correctness that people who see our good works will glorify "our Father Who is in heaven" (Matt. 5,16). Just as a good child becomes the reason that its father is honored and glorified, in the same way a true Christian honors and glorifies the Father. Whereas a Christian who lives an unchristian life, becomes a cause for atheists and impious people to defame the faith and blaspheme God. "Hallowed," therefore, means "Glorified."

The second petition is "Thy Kingdom Come." We ask for His Kingdom to come. But how? you ask. God does not reign in the world. We answer. The world is divided into a material realm and a spiritual realm. The material realm consists of the earth, the sun, the moon, comets, galaxies, the millions and billions of stars. For all these God has put what are called natural laws and with these He rules the universe. Everything obeys God. There is no clock that works with the accuracy with which the natural world works. Without this order and precision, without constant divine direction, without divine providence, the universe would have dissolved and been destroyed.

But inside this natural universe there is a creature which, while it enjoys all of the blessings of God and should for this reason all the more, of all the creatures, obey and submit itself to God, opposes Him and says: No! to God. That creature is man.

The great majority of peole do not want the Kingdom of God. They move out of divine law and the moral track which God has drawn for their harmonious life and living together with other things and people *(symbiosis)*. In them, Christ does not reign. The Anti-Christ reigns.

If we look at the whole globe, we will see that two-thirds of humanity are far from Christianity and believe in doctrines foreign to and even contrary to the true faith. In many places, which are governed by atheistic and totalitarian regimes, the Church is severely persecuted. But also in the Christian world, if we take a look, we shall see that many of those who are called Christians have ceased to be connected spiritually with Christ and live a life of apostasy, a life worse than the one the idolaters lived.

In all those people Christ does not reign. Because Christ does not want to make followers by force.

Nevertheless, the Kingdom of Christ exists like a small flock. To it belong those who believe and live according to the will of God. Our conviction is that some day the Kingdom of Christ shall be victorious over all the satanic obstacles everywhere on earth.

The second petition of the Lord's Prayer expresses this wish: "Thy Kingdom come."

"THY WILL BE DONE..."

"GIVE US THIS DAY OUR DAILY BREAD..."

We continue the interpretation of the "Lord's Prayer." We are at the third petition, at "Thy will be done on earth as it is in heaven."

God's will is expressed first by conscience, which is called the voice of God. If a person listened to the voice of conscience, he would not have need of the written law. Because, however, man sinned and his whole internal world was darkened, the voice of conscience could not be heard clearly. Exactly as when a storm occurs the voice of the rooster is not heard, in the same way in the storm which is caused by human passions the voice of conscience cannot be clearly heard.

For this reason the Lord revealed His will with the written law. That written law was the Ten Commandments given in the beginning. But a perfect written law is the Bible.

Conscience, the Ten Commandments, the Bible are means which express God's will. And to those who believe in Christ, besides the knowledge of the will of God, is given grace, the strength that is to say, which, as we have said other times, derives from Christ's sacrifice on the Cross. The Gospel does not only say: "Do this and that," but gives also the power of grace, which enables even the most sinful person to come out of the swamp of sin and be elevated to heights of virtue that are hard to contemplate. With grace, from a wild beast, man can become an angel.

That this is a reality, the history of the Church testifies when it presents us with a multitude of men and women who believed in Christ, received His grace, left their sinful past and realized here on earth an angelic life.

The will of God is known today to us Christians. Known, as well, are the examples of the saints, who led beautiful lives. But while these are known, the world, the modern world, is influenced by various streams of unbelief and sin, and does not do the will of the heavenly Father. It follows the wills of sinful people whom it honors and glorifies as leaders and teachers of human life. It is deceived by and dazzled by their slogans and theories and continuously goes away from God.

Most people do the will of satan, and doing satan's will sink in the swamp of misery. The ideal society, which they desire to see, the Kingdom of God, remains far from this world.

But there is another world, where the will of God is performed with eagerness and zeal, and because of this a certain amount of order and harmony reign in our world. It is the world of the holy angels and archangels. And if we people – who potentially do not differ much from the angels, for we were created free and reasonable beings – wished to imitate the example of the angels and with all our hearts did the will of God, then here on earth would come the Kingdom of God. Earth would become heaven. Righteousness, peace, and love would reign here. War would not exist.... Unfortunately, though, the will of God is not done. And for this reason unbearable misery and misfortune prevail on earth. Earth becomes hell, a prelude, the beginning of hell.

But those who believe in Christ and know the paradise that the faithful performance of the will of God brings, groan for the contemporary misfortune of humanity. They address themselves to the heavenly Father, expressing their wish that the will of God prevail, by saying: "Thy will be done on earth as it is in heaven."

And now we come to the fourth petition of the Lord's Prayer. That petition is: "Give us this day our daily bread." Our Father, we ask Thee, give us our bread, the everyday and necessary bread.

Man, my dear ones, is not only soul. If he were only soul, he would not have any need of material things. He would live like an angel, without material needs. But man is a composite being, he is soul and body. And the body has material needs. Man hungers, thirsts, feels cold, and has the need for clothing, housing and medicines for his illnesses. No matter how much someone may limit his material needs and is willing to live like an ascetic, he will still have the need for bread (food) and water. All these needs are expressed by the words "daily bread."

"Our daily bread." Unfortunately, man does not limit himself to the necessities of life. To these he has added and is adding other things, many of which are harmful, others useless, and a few are those which give some benefit and beauty to life. Thus man is driven away from the daily bread, and by his useless and harmful "needs" he has created a new situation. He has created a new society, which is called "a consuming society," a society which is considered progressive and civilized when it consumes much for its needs.

But such a society cannot last long. As history teaches, the time of the "fat cows" will be succeeded by the time of the "thin cows." The time will come, that is to say, when humanity will feel not only the lack of useless things, but the lack of the most necessary things, as are bread and water. And like the prodigal son it shall cry: "I perish with hunger" (Luke 15,17), i.e. I am starving to death!

But saying this petition of ours in the Lord's Prayer, let us pay attention again to the word "our." That word means that we must not concern ourselves only for our own daily bread, but we must also concern ourselves for the daily bread of other people. It is not right that one be full and another hunger. And we must not only pray, but we must also fight against the injustices of the world, which make so many people lack food. It is estimated that the amount of money spent by one man in the rich nations, the so-called consuming societies, is enough to feed a hundred people in the under-developed nations, where thousands of people die from hunger every day. Thus, we must concern ourselves for the "daily bread" not of the few, but of all.

"...AS WE FORGIVE THOSE WHO TRESPASS AGAINST US"

In our interpretation of the Lord's Prayer, we had come to the fourth petition, but before going any further, we should answer a question: Why is the Lord's Prayer included in the Divine Liturgy? Whatever is said and done in the Liturgy is done with a purpose, and the Lord's Prayer, said after the Consecration of the Precious Gifts, serves a purpose. According to the Teachers and Fathers of the Church, the request for "our daily bread," is mentioned, because by this we ask not only for ordinary bread, but also for spiritual food. By saying, "our daily bread," we direct our thoughts to that other bread, the bread which came down from heaven, our Lord Jesus Christ. This bread is now on the Holy Table. Christ Himself said: "I am the living bread which came down from heaven: if any man eat of this bread, he shall live forever: and the bread that I will give is my flesh, which I will give for the life of the world" (John 6:51). The flesh about which Christ speaks is *Holy Communion.*

By saying "give us this day our daily bread" at this point in the Divine Liturgy, we are asking our heavenly Father to give us two kinds of bread, earthly and heavenly. The first is indeed necessary, but the second is incomparably more necessary.

And now let us look at the fifth petition of the Lord's Prayer: "And forgive us our trespasses, as we forgive those who trespass against us."

No one on earth is free of sin; we sin daily. We sin with deeds, with words, and with thoughts. Everyone who fights against sin and puts a lot of effort into not sinning, eventually gets caught in a web of sinful thoughts. And even one evil thought will begin to pollute us morally, if allowed to penetrate our minds.

Sins which we commit are symbolized in the Gospel as debts. That is to say, every time we sin, an unseen hand writes the sin on our books, that is in our soul, putting us in debt. In very little time, then, our Book of life has gathered a debt from our sinful thoughts, words and deeds. This debt is enormous, and by ourselves, we cannot pay it off. According to the Law of justice, we should be condemned and put into prison, hell, eternally. But God's mercy comes -- the Blood of the God-Man -- erasing all this debt. And we who believe and are baptized in the name of Christ are finally delivered from the weight and guilt of sin.

We *should not* sin after being baptized. However, we do. In ancient times, when people were baptized at an older age, some sinned more after Baptism than before. Then Christians appeared preaching that only those sins committed before Baptism were forgiven. Serious sins committed after Baptism were regarded unforgivable, and it was held that anyone who sinned should be excommunicated. But this view was condemned by the Church as a heresy, for God's mercy is an endless ocean. The Church argued that His mercy extends not only to sin committed before Baptism, but after it as well.

The fifth petition of the Lord's Prayer also testifies to this: if God had closed the door of His mercy after Baptism, why then should we kneel and ask for forgiveness of sins committed every day? Our Father, forgive us our debts, we beg You. We cannot be calm and peaceful inside, for the voice of our conscience testifies that we did not keep Your will, and have sinned against You, the all-merciful God. Our Father, forgive us.

And what does our heavenly Father answer? He answers in the Gospel of His Son, that forgiveness of sins is easy. It is given to us *if* we forgive the sins of others who wronged us and made us unhappy. Forgive the sins of your fellow man, in order that God may forgive your sins. Is it difficult? Animosity in our souls makes it so difficult that we do not want to forgive others, even in the last moments of their lives. We are cruel and uncharitable, but the lord is merciful and kind.

In spite of the difficulty our egos present, it is beneficial for us to forgive. Think for a minute! Suppose you owed someone a million dollars, and he was willing to erase all that debt on the condition that you erase the debt of one dollar that someone else owes you. We would be insane to refuse such an offer! This is how great the difference is between the debt we owe God and the debts others owe us.

Brothers and sisters, forgive if you want to be forgiven. Imitate Christ, Who taught us to forgive not only in theory, but in practice as well. Christ embraced all humanity on the Cross, and he prayed for His enemies, saying: "Father, forgive them; for they do not know what they are doing" (Luke 23:24).

"AND LEAD US NOT INTO TEMPTATION"

We continue our interpretation of the Lord's Prayer. The sixth petition is: "And lead us not into temptation." That is, "We ask You, O heavenly Father, not to let us be tempted."

First of all, let us see what temptation is. Temptation is a *testing* of our love and obedience to God's will. We are tempted all our lives. There come occasions to sin. During this battle, will we be defeated?

Let us take an example to give us a more vivid picture of the situation of temptation: A ship is sailing over the ocean. The weather is fine, no wind is blowing, no waves. The sea looks like a mirror under the rays of the sun. After a while, however, the weather changes. The wind blows, and gets ever stronger, creating huge waves. Now the ship is in danger. Will she pass through the waves, or be brought down by them? The captain on the deck is vigilant. He is watchful because with one wrong move, the ship would sink. The ship is being tested, but more than that, the abilities and skill of the captain are being tried. A good captain is never seen when the sea is calm, but only when it is troubled.

What happens on the sea is an image of what happens to us in society. Life in this world is like the sea, and this sea is sometimes calm, sometimes troubled. Evil, like a huge wave, comes to strike our ship, i.e. our existence; our physical and, moreover, our spiritual existence. The waves which rise so strong, that we fear sinking, spiritually.

Winds, storms and tempests come into our lives. We have to be careful, like the captain in the storm. Evil is all around us.

Where does evil come from? God does not cause evil. God "cannot be tempted," as St. James says, He is above evil, above sin (James 1:13). It is a sin to say that sin, which is evil, has its source in God.

Evil comes from us, from the bad use of our reason and freedom given us by our gracious God. Evil comes from humanity's distorted nature, because we are not as we were when we came out of God's hand. Humanity preferred evil, sin, and became perverted. Evil became rooted in human hearts and transmitted from one generation to another. A heavy inheritance grasps mankind. The faults and vices of our ancestors have created an inclination to sin, and everybody has it in their hearts. From our hearts, like a troubled sea, temptations come, and do not stop bothering us as long as we live here on earth. We should be very careful to repel these temptations, which start out as small waves, like passing thoughts, but later get bigger and bigger, like tidal waves, and our ship is in danger of sinking.

A part of our temptations comes from other people who do not live according to God's will and provoke us to evil by what they say and do. These people, even if they may be very close to us and say they are concerned for our good, can become temptations, and even great temptations. Think of Job's wife: She became the biggest temptation in his life, for she was tempting him to blaspheme God and commit suicide. But Job overcame this temptation which came through his wife.

Temptation is our evil desire, our distorted ego. Temptation is our fellow man, who, by their anti-Christian ideas, constitute a whole world of error and sin.

There is yet a third source of temptation, coming neither from ourselves nor from other human beings. It comes from the devil. The devil never stops taking advantage of every situation to tempt and disquiet the waters, creating storms and tempests.

Therefore, bringing back the image we mentioned at the beginning, we are continually on troubled waters, tempted from all sides and in danger of sinning, if we are not heedful – and most important – if, because of ourselves, we lose God's help. Our merciful and loving God never stops caring for us and is ever ready to help us in our difficult journey. It is enough just to say: "My God, I want You to help me overcome this temptation."

The question is: Do we want to overcome temptations? If we want to, we should avoid them. We should avoid anything that causes us to sin. Today, in addition to everything else that stirs up the fires of temptation, pushing us toward evil, we have shameful magazines, and books written by atheistic and materialistic journalists and authors; there are shameful shows playing at theatres, movies and television; there are night clubs; there are bad friendships. . . .

Unfortunately, however, instead of avoiding these sources and defeating temptation, we fall into them, defeated and dishonored. We do not resist. We do not fight. We do not say what Christ said in a similar situation: "Get thee hence, Satan" (Matt. 4:10). We go to satan ourselves. We throw ourselves over the precipice, and then – O our mockery of sacred things! – we pray: "Lead us not into temptation."

"BUT DELIVER US FROM THE EVIL ONE"

We have come to the seventh and last petition of the Lord's Prayer. It says: "But deliver us from the evil one." That is to say: "Heavenly Father, we ask You to save us from the wicked devil who constantly fights against us."

People today, for the most part, pretending to be progressive and modern, laugh when someone mentions the devil. They contend that there is no devil. How do we answer them? We could answer in many ways, but in this short homily, we will say only a few words.

If we deny the existence of the devil, we cannot explain the existence of evil in man and in the world. If there is no devil, then where does evil come from? From God? But it is not logical for God to be the cause of evil, as we explained in our preceding homily; it is out of the question. God does not tempt. He is the source of all good things. Neither could evil originate with mankind, because evil would then be incurable.

The first evil came from "outside." It came from another being who discovered and spread evil, and this being is the devil. He is an incorporeal being, a fallen archangel. He conceived evil; was overcome with pride; turned away from God, the source of Good; and from the heights, he fell into the chaos of evil and corruption. He turned his light into darkness; he enclosed himself in evil, hatred against God and mankind. He hates and envies us, because we stayed faithful to God's will.

Hating us, the devil never ceases to fight us, attempting to lead us into evil. He uses many means. Being evil and corrupt himself, he never presents himself the way he really is, for if he did, as the wild and sinister being he is, we would avoid encountering him as we would snakes and wild animals. As the Apostle Paul says, he appears in the form of a luminous angel. He is the Great Deceiver. He approaches us, pretending to be our friend; he tries to be social with us; he tries to tell us what is good for us. Honey flows from his lips, but it is honey mixed with poison. In this way he deceived Eve, saying that by disobeying God's commandment, not only would nothing happen to her, but she and her husband would become gods – gods obeying the devil!

As a spirit, satan, the devil, follows us and learns our weaknesses from various happenings, and according to our inclinations, he plans his strategy. For each of us, he has the proper bait. . . . If one leans toward gluttony, he tries to win him with delicious meals, plenty of wine, and rich foods. If one likes money, he will suggest various means of becoming a millionaire. Another, who likes pleasures and amusements, he will try to win with corrupt women, who will drain him of his money and his life. Another, who likes fame and glory, and is carried away by empty praise and dignities. . . .

Satan tempts everyone. He leaves no one untouched – as we see in the Gospel, he even went into the desert to tempt our Lord Jesus Christ. He showed Him all the kingdoms of the earth with their glories. He told Him that all would be His, and was ready to give them, if Christ would fall down and worship him. But Christ sent him away, saying: "Get thee hence, Satan: for it is written, Thou shalt worship the Lord thy God, and him only shalt thou serve" (Matt. 4:10). Christ defeated satan, and angels came to minister to Him.

But when we say, "deliver us from evil," we not only accept the existence of the devil and the many m.ans he uses to defeat us, but we also recognize that ⁄e are weak.

It is impossible for us to defeat the devil. If we were able to conquer him and be freed of evil, Christ would not have come to earth. But Christ came to fight and vanquish the devil, to liberate us from the bonds of sin. Christ defeated the devil in the desert, and defeated him again on Golgotha. There, the devil put up the worst battle and was vanquished and disgraced, and since then, Christ giv es His power to us to defeat the devil.

To which people is this given? To those who believe in God, who believe that He is King and Redeemer of the world, and who are eager to do His commandments. They receive unseen power from Christ to defeat the devil completely. And with Christ, the weak person becomes strong.

We can see this clearly in the lives of the Saints. The Apostle Peter became proud, and because of this, God's grace left him and he was defeated by the devil. But when Peter came to his senses, understood his sin and repented, he shed bitter tears, and Christ forgave him. Peter came in touch with Christ, the Conqueror of sin and evil, and Peter defeated the devil.

If we are distant from Christ, we are very weak, but close to Him, we receive tremendous power to defeat every temptation.

Dear friends in Christ, one who accepts these truths about the devil's existence, and the means the devil uses to defeat us, knows that he cannot confront these temptations by himself. So he kneels contritely before God and asks for His help: "And lead us not into temptation, but deliver us from evil."

And Christ, hearing this prayer, protects him. He sends an angel to guard him, and even when he treads on dangerous ground, He saves him from the cliffs and chasms. He is his Lord, the Conqueror of sin and death.

HOLY COMMUNION

VIII

HOLY COMMUNION

NOT SLAVES, BUT FREE

After the Lord's Prayer, the priest exclaims: "For Thine is the Kingdom and the power and the glory, of the Father and of the Son and of the Holy Spirit, now and forever, and from all ages to all ages."

This exclamation is the explanation given for all that we asked in the Lord's prayer. What did we ask for? We asked for the sanctification of God's name, the Kingdom of God, the establishment of God's will on earth as it is in heaven, our daily bread, the forgiveness of sins, the avoidance of temptation, and our redemption from satan's traps. We asked for all these things because we believe that the One to whom we are speaking is the King of the Universe, the Almighty and glorious One, from whom every good thing comes. He is the triune God: Father, Son and Holy Spirit. It is to Him we sinners go for refuge.

Without this belief, an unshaken faith in the triune God, our prayer cannot have miraculous results. In other times, when this faith existed, the Lord's Prayer was not said by the cantor alone, but by all the people – and with such contrition and fervor that one would think himself transported to heaven. Indeed, earth used to become heaven and people, like holy angels and archangels, praised and glorified God. In the Russian Church in times past, when the Lord's Prayer was said, everyone knelt.

May those vibrant years of worshipping God "in spirit" (John 4:24) again come with our efforts, particularly those of the priests.

After this "explanation," and the loud "Amen" of the people, the priest turns to the people and says, "Peace be with you." And the people return: "And with thy spirit." That is to say: "May this hour prevail in the souls of all, priests and laymen. No passion, no thought of disbelief, no sin should disturb the inner being of our souls. We should all be like untroubled waters – we should have calmness of soul.

After the "Peace be with you," the deacon or priest commands the congregation and himself: "Let us bow our heads to the Lord." This command is followed by the following prayer:

"We give thanks to Thee, O King Invisible, who by Thy boundless power hast formed all things and by the fullness of Thy mercy hast brought forth all things out of nothingness into being. Do Thou Thyself, O Master, look down from heaven upon those who have bowed down their heads before Thee; for they have bowed not before flesh and blood, but before Thee, Almighty God. Do Thou, therefore, O Master, administer these offerings to all of us for good, according to the special need of each of us; do Thou travel with those that travel, by land, by water or by air; and do Thou, Physician of our souls and bodies, heal those of us who are sick."

With this beautiful prayer, we express our gratitude to God. We are reminded that God created everything in His immense power, and brought everything to life. God, having created the world out of nothing, performs an even greater miracle in the Divine Liturgy: He changes the bread and wine into Christ's Body and Blood.

We are captivated by the divine creation, but we are more ecstatic at the Divine Eucharist. God's grandeur is boundless in both cases; therefore, we bow our heads before God.

We do not bow before mere men, be they great or powerful, but we do bow our heads before the awesome God. Awesome God, we entreat You at this time to help us. Clear difficulties and obstacles away from our lives; give us what we need for our physical and spiritual existence; travel with those who travel, being a wayfarer with them; console and give courage to the sick, for You are the Physician of our souls and bodies.

"Let us bow our heads unto the Lord." An egotistic unbeliever, hearing this liturgical command would be scandalized and say that religion degrades the human personality, that it cultivates a spirit of fear and slavery which was tolerable in times past, but in today's age of freedom, it has no place.

What do we answer? Those who have such an opinion also have a misunderstanding of our religion, because our religion is one of freedom. No one emphasized human liberty as much as Christ; but unfortunately, we make bad choices. We choose evil, and this becomes slavery to wickedness and vice, slavery to the devil. While the political system of our governments may be liberal and democratic, and we consider ourselves free, in the area of inner freedom, the most important kind of liberty, we are not masters, but slaves and captives. Great tyrants, inner tyrants, our sinful passions, distress and torture humanity; they suck our sweat and blood like leeches, and we serve them. Christ said, "Whoever committeth sin is a servant of sin" (John 8:34).

Those of us who are enslaved to these inner tyrants,

the passions, are easily subjugated to external ones. For this reason, we see people who boast that they are free falling down in veneration before great and powerful men, just as the slaves of ancient times used to venerate their masters.

But Christians (not nominal Christians, but those who truly believe and live according to the will of Christ) are really free. They do not work for evil and vice. Christ reigns in their heart, the Liberator and Redeemer of the World, who frees us by his precious blood, and who wants us to be free.

True Christians stand before men. They do not bow to anyone, no matter how powerful they are, but they bow to Christ, lowering their heads and worshipping Him in thankfulness.

Christians kneel before God, but stand before men. This is real freedom, as in the liturgical command: "Let us bow our heads unto the Lord."

"HOLY THINGS UNTO THE HOLY"

Dear friends, the Mystery has been completed. Clergy and laity are preparing to receive Holy Communion. In connection with this preparation is another new prayer which the priest addresses to our Lord Jesus Christ. It is:

"Hearken, O Lord Jesus Christ our God, from Thy holy dwelling place and from the throne of glory of Thy Kingdom, and come and sanctify us, Thou Who sittest above with the Father and art here invisibly present with us, and do Thou deign by Thy mighty power to give us of Thy sacred Body and of Thy precious Blood, and through us to all the people."

With this prayer, the priest asks Christ to listen to our prayers. You, O Christ, Who are in heaven and sit on the throne of glory, overseeing and governing the universe, You are sitting together with the Father, but are also here in the Divine Liturgy, we ask You to come and make us holy. With Your invisible hand, we ask You to give to us, the priests, Your holy body and Blood, and with our hands, give them to all Your people.

After this beautiful prayer, the priest exhorts: "Let us attend." That is to say, our Church is calling us to pay attention. The moment is holy: the priest takes the consecrated Bread from the paten, elevates it and says: "Holy things unto the holy." We will now say a few words about these last words of the priest.

First of all, why does the priest elevate (raise) the Bread? First, because he is about to unite it with the Holy Blood in the Chalice; and second, because he wants to show our lord Jesus Christ, Who was crucified, Who descended into Hades for the souls of the dead, destroyed the power of darkness, and after three days rose in eternal triumph. The elevation is a symbolic representation of the Lord's resurrection from the dead.

What does "Holy things unto the holy" mean? The Holy Things are the Body and Blood of Christ – priceless pearls. These Holy Things are given to the Saints. Not all Christians are saints. We explained in another homily what "saint" means. The question is now raised, "are we saints?" Are we worthy of being given the Holy Mysteries?

We answer: all of us are sinners; and, as Scripture says, there is not one day when we do not sin. Sin, as St. Macarios of Egypt said, is like a strong wind, which blows into a forest and shakes all the leaves on the trees. No leaf remains unshaken. Thus, no soul remains unshaken when it comes to sin. Sin is like a fine dust, which, even when the windows are closed, penetrates the house and lands on the furniture. Sin is like the sand of the Sahara, which, when strong winds blow, even comes through the closed windows of trains. Sin is like an unseen germ which gets into our systems and tries to subdue our bodies.

O sin! As thoughts and desires continuously penetrate unwatchful souls, they do not remain pure. But who is so careful that he avoids the infection caused by evil thoughts and desires? Evil thoughts and desires, according to Christ, are similar to actually commiting the sin. For example, a man who looks at a woman with lust, mentally commits adultery with her; another who hates his brother is mentally his brother's murderer!

In this way, we are all sinners, men and women, young and old, rich and poor, wise and ignorant, those who live in the world and those who left it to become ascetics. And just as there is no island that is untouched by the sea, there is no one who is not attacked on all sides by sin like a turbulent sea. We are all sinners. We are all guilty before God, all deserving eternal death.

Among the millions and billions of people who live on this planet, only one was without sin. He did not commit any sin; He never said an evil word; He thought no evil thoughts. His life was pure as the snow on untrodden mountaintops. He was holy, not in a relative sense, but in the absolute sense, and this man was our Lord Jesus Christ. He was holy, sinless, because he was not a mere man, but the God-Man. Being God, it was impossible for Him to sin. Because he was sinless, He offered himself as a sacrifice, and by this sacrifice the human race was forgiven. The precious blood he shed on the Cross, which is offered in the Divine Liturgy, cleanses us from every sin, and, as we said before, one drop of Christ's blood becomes a sea, an ocean in which millions of believers are washed and cleaned. Without this redemptive sacrifice of Christ, no one can be saved, no matter how many good works he does or how holily he acts.

Christians who are about to receive Holy Communion feel their sinfulness very deeply. With contrition, they look at Christ, the Sun of Righteousness, acknowledge their sinfulness, and, answering the exclamation of the priest, "Holy Things unto the holy," say: "One is holy, one is Lord, Jesus Christ, to the glory of God the Father. Amen."

Our Christ, You alone are holy. We are sinners, but sinners, who in spite of our sinfulness and imperfection, desire holiness and that perfect life which You led on earth. We ask You, the Sun of Righteousness, to send Your beams to illumine and sanctify us, that we may become little suns in this world, manifesting Your holiness and glory.

THE INDIVISIBLE

After the "One is holy...," the so-called Communion Hymn is sung, which on most Sundays is: "Praise ye the Lord from the heavens. Alleluia." In the Liturgy of the presanctified Gifts, we chant: "Taste and see how good the Lord is. Alleluia."

While the Communion Hymn is being chanted and the Beautiful Gate is closed, the priest prepares to receive Holy Communion in the Holy Sanctuary. Therefore, at the deacon's instruction, "Master, break the Holy Bread," the priest says, "The Lamb of God is broken and distributed; broken but not sundered, always fed upon and never consumed, but sanctifying those who partake." He takes the Holy Bread, breaks it into four parts, so that there is a stamp on each one: IC on the first, XC on the second, NI on the third, and KA on the fourth. When we connect these letters, they form the sentence, IHCOYC XPICTOC NIKA, "Jesus Christ conquers." This is a declaration of our faith, that Christ, as God-Man, is invincible. No power can defeat faith in Christ. Christ conquers and triumphs forever; and blessed are those who have no doubt in their hearts, but believe like the first Christians did. They used to receive Holy Communion with great reverence.

"The Lamb of God is broken and distributed." By breaking the Bread, the priest imitates Christ. When He performed the Mystery of Mysteries for the first time,

Christ took the bread, broke it into small pieces, and gave one piece to each of His Apostles. Even though the Holy Bread is broken into pieces, even though it is broken into billions of pieces in all the Holy Sanctuaries of Orthodoxy, the heavenly Bread, the Body of Christ, the Lamb of God remains unsundered, i.e. one and only one.

How does this happen? It is a mystery that we cannot understand. If the sea could be contained in a water glass, then every divine mystery would fit into our brains. We believe what our Church testifies, which is, that the Holy Bread, though continuously broken, remains undiminshed.

To give an idea of this mystery, let's mention what a great theologian of our time once said. It is the example of the sun. The sun burns continuously, every day – every hour – it sends countless billions of rays to earth, light and heat. Every ray is certainly a small thing for the sun. Though it sends countless rays, it always remains the same. Science most certainly assures us that one day the sun will burn up, but the sun now seems unchangeable for us.

In spite of the everyday drain on the sun, it remains the same. A remarkable phenomenon. This is a small example to show us that Christ, the resplendent Sun, is whole on all the sacred Altars throughout the ages; Christ's Holy Body itself remains unsundered. It is distributed, but does not exhaust itself, like a sun which can spread its rays without end; like a river which flows endlessly, and its waters never dry up.

Christ, in order to show that his Body of bread is never exhausted, took five loaves of bread into the wilderness, and with them fed five thousand men (not counting women or children). Let us bow our heads humbly before the divine Majesty and with contrite heart give thanks to the Lord for His priceless gift.

The priest does something else: to the request of the deacon, "Master, fill the Holy Chalice," the priest takes that piece of the Holy Bread on which is printed the IC, and places it in the Holy Chalice, saying: "The fullness of the Cup of Faith and of the Holy Spirit. Amen." The meaning of this is: "The Lord became man; He suffered and was crucified; He was buried and was resurrected; He ascended into the heavens, so that we could receive the Holy Spirit, who, like an inexhaustible river, began watering the Church after Christ's sacrifice on the Cross. Without this sacrifice, it was impossible for the Holy Spirit to come. Those who believe in Christ can feel it. For anyone else, these words, and even the entire Liturgy is incomprehensible.

"The fullness of the Cup of Faith and of the Holy Spirit." Placing the consecrated Bread into the Holy Chalice results in the union of the two elements, the consecrated Bread and Wine.

Finally, before the priest partakes of Holy Communion, he does one other thing: at the deacon's request, "Master, bless the holy Zeon," he pours boiling *(zeon)* water into the Chalice, saying: "Blessed is the ardor of Thy Saints, now and forever and unto Ages of Ages. Amen." Not cold water, but hot must be poured into the Chalice at this time. Why? Because, as we read in the Gospel, when a soldier pierced Christ's side with his lance, blood and water came out, a sign that He had died. To remember this event, the priest pours hot water into the Holy Chalice.

There is another reason why hot water is poured into the Chalice: Christians should always be fervent in their feelings toward Christ, but especially so before Holy Communion. The desire to partake of Holy Communion must be like fire burning within them.

Does this desire exist in the hearts of our clergy and laity? If it does, then a sign of souls that feel this is their preparation for Holy Communion. If, however, it is not there, then how do we dare, clergy and laity, to receive the Holy Mysteries? Cold hearts. . . .

O Lord, make our hearts fervent with Divine love, so that no one will receive Holy Communion coldly and indifferently.

WE ONLY TOUCH

In our last homily, we said that the priest does the following things before receiving Holy Communion: he first breaks the Lamb of God, that is to say, the consecrated Bread, into four pieces; he places one piece in the Holy Chalice; then, he pours hot water into the Chalice.

Now, he is about to receive Holy Communion, but before doing so, according to the Order of the Orthodox Church, the priest kneels before the Holy Table and reads prayers, which with their superb contents, aid in preparing him for the Sacrament. These prayers should be said not only by the priest, but by the laymen as well; therefore, they are copied below:

1. "I stand before the doors of Thy Sanctuary, yet I do not put away from me my hurtful thoughts; but Thou, O Christ our God, who didst justify the Publican, and have mercy upon the Canaanite woman, and open the gates of Paradise to the Thief, open also unto me the bounty of Thy compassion, and as I approach to touch Thee, receive me even as the Harlot and the Woman with the issue of blood. For the one by the mere touch of the hem of Thy garment was healed, and the other by clasping Thy sacred feet obtained release from her sins. And I, in my pitiableness, dare to receive Thy whole Body; let me not, therefore, be seared as by flame, but receive me even as these; enlighten the senses of my soul and purge as with fire the stains of my sins: through

the intercessions of her who in purity bore Thee, and of the heavenly powers; for Thou art blessed from all Ages to all Ages. Amen."

2. "I believe, O Lord, and confess that Thou art verily the Christ, the Son of the living God, who didst come into the world to save sinners, of whom I am the chief. Also I believe that this is Thy sacred Body and this, Thy precious Blood. Therefore I pray Thee, have mercy upon me and pardon my transgressions, voluntary and involuntary, in word and in deed, both known and unknown, and make me fit worthily to partake of Thy sacred Mysteries, unto the remission of sins and unto life everlasting. Amen."

3. "Behold, I approach for Holy Communion,
O Creator, burn me not as I partake,
For Thou art fire which burns the unworthy,
Wherefore do Thou cleanse me from every stain."

4. "Receive me today, O Son of God, as a partaker of Thy Mystic Feast; for I will not speak of Thy Mystery to Thine enemies; I will not kiss Thee as did Judas, but as the Thief I will confess Thee: Lord, remember me when Thou comest into Thy Kingdom."

5. "Tremble, O mortal, beholding the divine Blood.
For it is to the unworthy as a live coal.
The Body of God both deifies and nourishes me:
Deifies my soul and wondrously nourishes my mind."

6. "Thou has smitten me with yearning, O Christ, and with Thy divine love hast Thou changed me; but do Thou burn away with spiritual fire my sins and make me worthy to be filled with the joy of Thee; that rejoicing in Thy goodness I may magnify Thy two presences."

7. "Into the glorious company of Thy Saints how shall I, all unworthy, enter? For should I dare to go into the Festal Chamber, my robe betrays me, for it is not a festal garment and I shall be by the Angels bound and cast out. Cleanse my soul, O Lord, from pollution, and of Thy compassion save me."

8. "O Merciful Master, Lord Jesus Christ my God, let not these Holy Things be unto me for judgement through my unworthiness, but rather for the purification and sanctification of my soul and body, and as an earnest of the Life and Kingdom to come. For it is good for me to cling to my God and place in the Lord my hope of salvation."

4. "Receive me today, O Son of God, as a partaker of Thy Mystic Feast; for I will not speak of Thy Mystery to Thine enemies; I will not kiss Thee as did Judas, but as the Thief I will confess Thee: Lord, remember me when Thou comest into Thy Kingdom."

Should we explain these prayers word-for-word? I do not think it is necessary, because the faithful who receive Holy Communion often repeat these same prayers, and repetition makes them the property of every pious soul. In spite of the archaic language and the fact that some cannot understand the deep meaning behind each word, they say them repeatedly, so that they know them by heart and can say them, not indifferently, but with deep contrition.

These prayers express unshaken faith and fervent love for our Lord Jesus Christ. They confess our weakness and sinfulness which make us tremble when we are before the Divine Mystery.

In addition, they confess that, even at this holy moment, the tempter does not leave us alone, but tries to trouble us with terrible thoughts, to take away our peace of soul and lead us away from Holy Communion. What a state of mind! It is enough to say that some pious souls who are unhindered and ready to receive Holy Communion, do not do so at the very last minute because their souls are troubled by evil and shameful thoughts, which the devil has successfully planted there. And these poor people think that these thoughts, which came from the outside like birds of prey, are their own thoughts, offspring of their own feelings.

O faithful, satan is the one who tempts you. Pay attention, chase satan away, and concentrate on your prayers. Put all your hope in the boundless mercy and infinite love of Christ. Christ is an ocean of love and mercy. There were two women in the Gospel, one with an issue of blood and the other, a sinful woman. The first touched Christ's garment and the other clasped and kissed His feet. They did not burn, but received Divine grace abundantly, and left satisfied with His boundless mercy. These two women give us courage and fear as well. For when we receive Holy Communion, we do not merely touch Christ as these women did, but we receive the whole of Him into our hearts.

How clean this heart should be! How it should shine! The garments of our souls should be clean and shining as we are about to come near to the Divine Feast and receive the Holy Mysteries.

O Christ, I feel I am a sinner and unworthy to receive You, the pure and undefiled One. I do not dare gaze at the divine glory of Your Feast. But not receive Holy Communion? Then, I will violate Your divine command.

Receive it then? I fear and tremble because of my filthiness. "I do not have a garment, sweet Bridegroom, to enter Your bridal chamber."

Fear, but aspiration too, should abide in the souls of everyone who receives Holy Communion.

After these moving prayers, the priests draw near and partake of the Holy Mysteries.

O Lord, may all our clergy, realizing the importance of the moment they receive Holy Communion, receive it worthily. Let none partake as did Judas, but always have the prayer of the grateful thief on their lips and in their hearts: "Lord, remember me when Thou comest into Thy Kingdom" (Luke 23:42).

THE INVITATION

In ancient times, the first centuries of Christianity, after the priests received Communion, the laymen entered the Holy Bema and also received it. They used to receive it the same way the clergy did, i.e. separately – the Holy Body first, then the Precious Blood.

Later on, however, the custom developed where only the clergy received Holy Communion separately, and the laymen received it together in the Chalice. Therefore, after receiving Holy Communion, the priest, holding the Chalice reverently, comes out through the Beautiful Gate and addreses the people: "With fear of God, with faith and with love draw near."

These words constitute an invitation to the congregation to come and receive the Holy Mysteries. In olden times, when Christians had living faith and lived according to God's will, everyone in the church would come at this time and partake of Holy Communion. But later, ignorance and darkness came to our nations. Faith cooled, morals weakened, and Christians did not receive Holy Communion as before. The invitation, "With fear of God, with faith and with love draw near," continued to be uttered, but it was said mechanically, with neither the laymen nor the priest understanding what the words meant.

It therefore became rare for a Christian to receive Communion on Sundays. In fact, it is said that once a pious Christian heard the invitation "With fear of God . . . ," and came up to receive Communion. The priest was amazed and did not want to give it, saying that only on Easter and Christmas do people receive Holy Communion! Easter and Christmas? Then, why invite us at every Liturgy to draw near and partake? Imagine the ignorance! A priest hindering prepared Christians from receiving the Sacraments! Divine Liturgy without anyone receiving Holy Communion is an offense and insult to Him who prepared the Table and invited Christians to draw near!

Yes, Christians should receive the Sacraments. But how? Here, the invitation itself is important, for it is not enough for Christians to receive the Sacraments, but they must receive them with fear of God, with faith and love.

First of all, we should approach with the fear of God. What is fear of God? It is the noble feeling of reverence and contrition which should overflow in the Christian heart when he considers the boundless abyss that separates him from God, when he considers God's immense condescension when He became man to make man like God. If the Cherubim and Seraphim stand with fear before God and cover their faces, how much more should we stand with fear before the Holy Table?

The way we approach the Sacraments shows if we have the fear of God in our hearts. Unfortunately, when we observe the way Christians come to partake of Holy Communion, on the great feasts of Christmas and Easter, we cry for our situation. They gather before the Beautiful Gate, push and shove; they are in a hurry to be first. They create such a disturbance, that in some communities, priests are forced to put up an iron fence, because they are afraid the rush of people will upset the Holy Chalice, spilling the Precious Blood of Christ – considered a terrible accident. No one stands in a corner of the church saying, 'I will receive Communion last.'

It is related of a heroic general that, when time came to receive Holy Communion, everyone offered him his place in line; but the pious general did not consent. He said that in the Church there is no discrimination; we are all sinners and equals before God.... And realizing his sinfulness, he received Holy Communion last of all. This example should be followed by all our Christians – not first, but last. Not even half an hour will pass until your turn comes.

You should receive Holy Communion with fear of God, but you must also receive the Sacraments with faith. What is faith? Not a vague faith in a higher power governing the universe, but a concrete faith, as is the faith which we confess in the Creed. Belief in the Holy Trinity, belief in Christ the Savior, belief in the Great Mystery of Holy Eucharist. There should be no doubt in the heart that receives Holy Communion that it is Christ's Body and Blood.

God is all-wise and omnipotent. He makes coal into diamonds. He makes water into sweet juice in the fruits of the trees. He acts upon and changes everything.

A certain ancient teacher of the Church used to say: O man, if you look at your entrails, you will find an example that will convince you of what God can do. Among the entrails, the teacher says, is the spleen. This is the organ that makes your blood. Considering this fact, he asks: "If the spleen, this simple organ, has the power to make this change, doesn't the Holy Spirit have such a power?

O man, humble yourself before God. Submit your reason to faith, and with this faith draw near to receive Holy Communion.

Christians, you should receive the Sacraments with fear of God and with faith. You should also receive them with love, the noblest of all feelings. Love should reign in our souls at Holy Communion, love which can repeat the words of Christ and say: "Father, forgive them; for they know not what they do" (Luke 23:34).

Unfortunately, however, most people do not receive Communion with love. These are like the man who kept the fast, and went to receive Communion on Easter; but when he saw his enemy in church, he was so disturbed that he forgot where he was and pulled a knife to kill him. And he would have killed him, if others had not stopped him. Hard hearts which do not even melt before the divine fire of God's boundless love!

People without the fear of God, without faith in the Mystery, and without love for their neighbors are unworthy to receive Holy Communion.

COME UNTO ME, ALL YE THAT LABOUR AND ARE HEAVY LADEN, AND I WILL GIVE YOU REST.
MATTHEW 11:28

"WE HAVE SEEN THE LIGHT..."

Dear friends, as we saw in our last homily, the priest, holding the Holy Chalice, comes through the Beautiful Gate and cries: "With the fear of God, with faith and with love, draw near." These words are an invitation which Christ offers through the priest to all the faithful in the church. All are invited to participate in the Mystical Supper. Everyone should draw near to receive Holy Communion, but do they all draw near, do they all participate?

When we see what is happening in our churches today, we notice that in almost every church, when the priest celebrates the Liturgy on a Sunday, only babies receive Holy Communion. Mothers carry their babies in their arms and bring them to receive Communion — a beautiful custom, of course — but babies do not need Holy Communion as much as adults, who experience sorrows and are attacked by satan that strives to conquer and enslave them.

Holy Communion is the most powerful weapon against temptation and sorrow, when Christians receive the Mysteries worthily. Unfortunately, however, they stay far away from Holy Communion, and, as a prayer of the Divine Service puts it, they are in danger of becoming the prey of the beast, that is, of falling into the mouth of the spiritual beast, satan, and being destroyed.

Adults do not approach the Chalice of Life, but they send infants to receive Holy Communion. They send them on Sundays and great feastdays. And when they start crying and screaming, they create such disorder in the church that the priests and cantors cannot be heard. It is forbidden to bring infants into movie houses and theatres, because people want absolute quiet so they can hear the devil's liturgy; but in church on Sundays and great holy days, there is great noise because of mothers and their babies.

What should be done? Shouldn't mothers bring their children to church? Shouldn't *they* at least receive the Holy Mysteries and be sanctified? We are not saying that mothers should not bring their infants. What we are saying is that there should be some order in the matter. Mothers should bring their babies to week-day Liturgies for Holy Communion. This was ordered by the Archbishop of Athens Chrysanthos, of blessed memory, and should be done by all priests.

Adults pay no attention to the invitation: "With fear of God...." They come up only on the great holy days, two or three times a year. They create great disorder, certainly a bigger one than infants, for the babies voices are innocent ones, while the whisperings, talk – and even quarrels – of adults around the Chalice is a great sin: it is desecration of the awesome Mystery!

Yes, Christians should receive Holy Eucharist, but how many times a year? If Christians are prepared, they should then receive Holy Communion; it is for this reason that the Liturgy is celebrated. The early Christians received Holy Communion often – every day!

What faith, piety and aspiration the early Christians had! Afterwards, however, ignorance and indifference kept Christians far from Holy Communion. They got into the habit of not receiving Communion, and they are keeping that habit. Therefore, priests and bishops have a great responsibility.

To those who ask how many times Christians should partake of Holy Communion, we give the answer of St. Chrysostom: "Are you prepared? Receive Holy Communion every day. Are you not prepared? Then don't receive it even on Easter!"

Why do we not prepare ourselves? Here is our sin. While it is easy to bathe and clean our bodies for the Holy Mystery, we are indifferent to the spiritual bath: repentance and confession.

Blessed are those souls who are in a state of repentance and confession, those who have experienced the pain of regret, cried for their sins, and made the steadfast decision not to sin again. With the permission of their Father Confessor, they come to partake of the Holy Mysteries. They receive Communion with fear and desire. They receive it as the invitation says: "with fear of God, with faith and with love."

On behalf of those who receive Holy Communion worthily, the cantor chants: "We have seen the true light; we have received the Heavenly Spirit; we have found the true Faith, worshiping the undivided Trinity, Who hath saved us."

What do these words mean? It is an expression of admiration for the great and lofty things which took place. It is said that in ancient times, when a Greek army had gone many miles in the desert, suffering from thirst, they saw the sea from a high hill, and their joy was so great that they all shouted, "The sea, the sea, we behold the sea!"

As people wandered in the wilderness of their passions and came to believe in Christ and received His

Holy Mysteries, they cried out in admiration of this precious gift, saying: "The light, the light." For Christ is light, His teaching is light, His sacrifice on the Cross is light, His resurrection is light. His Divine Liturgy, which is a representation of His life and sacrifice, is light. Holy Communion, which is in a mystical way Christ Himself, is light. They say — and it is no lie — that when faith was alive, Christians who came for Communion used to see the Holy Chalice shining like the sun. Those Christians were children of Light, children of the Church having radiant faces.

Unfortunately, however, we have left the era of light and have entered the era of moles — blind mice who do not like the light, living in tunnels underground. They never see the sun. These are the unbelievers and atheists. While Christ's light is shining from East to West lighting the whole universe, they do not want to come out of their dark tunnels.

But the faithful, those believers who go to church, attend the Divine Liturgy, receive the Holy Mysteries and are filled with enthusiasm, these cry aloud: "We have seen the light!"

WATER DRAWN UP ✝ UNTO LIFE EVERLASTING

"WE THANK THEE"

𝓐fter Holy Communion, while the hymn "We have seen the light..." is being chanted, the priest places the Chalice on the Holy Table and censes it, saying silently: "Be Thou exalted, O God, above the heavens and Thy glory above all the earth."

What do these words mean? We have said elsewhere that the Divine Liturgy is a re-enactment of the entire mystery of Divine Dispensation, that is to say, what God did for our salvation is re-performed in Divine Eucharist.

In the Liturgy, we hear the voices of the prophets who told of Christ's coming. We hear the angelic hymn: "Glory to God in the highest and on earth peace, good will toward men" (Luke 2:14). In the Prothesis we see a manger where Christ is born. At the Small Entrance, we see Christ who comes as a Teacher to preach His gospel. At the Great Entrance, we see Christ who comes this time as the High Priest to offer Himself as sacrifice for our salvation.

And now, when the sacrifice has been offered and Christians have received Holy Communion, we see Christ's Ascension. Raising the Holy Chalice with the priest's words, "Be Thou exalted, O God, above the heavens and Thy glory above all the earth," as if saying to Christ: You came down to earth from Your heavenly heights to find and save Your lost sheep. You humbled Yourself as no one else: You were born in a stable. Your first companions were animals, Your first breath was

the smell of a stable. You had no roof over Your head.
You walked and preached the gospel of Your Kingdom.
You faced obstacles. You were hated and persecuted by
Your enemies. You were sold for thirty coins. You were
judged and condemned to death. You were crucified.
You shed Your precious blood on Golgotha. You de-
scended into the dark kingdom of Hades. You preached
to the dead. After three days, You rose from the dead.

We have observed all these things during the
Liturgy. Here on earth once more, through the priest,
You offered us the Holy Service. And now we see You
in Your glorious Ascension, being raised up to heaven;
and from there You invite us to be raised up and become
citizens of heaven, where You reign forever. From earth
to heaven. What is an astronaut who goes through outer
space and lands on the moon? Christians are incomparably superior – through faith they become spiritual
astronauts, ascend into heaven, and become like the
angels.

We then hear the priest's command: "Let us rise.
Having duly received the divine, holy, pure, immortal,
heavenly, life-giving and awesome Mysteries of Christ,
worthily let us give thanks unto the Lord."

"Let us rise!" Why standing? In the ancient Church,
when all the faithful used to receive Holy Communion,
some time was needed for everyone to partake, and during this time, until the very last Christian received the
Sacraments, the faithful would be seated. Then, there
was order. Today, there is disorder. And when the priest
sees many people approaching for Holy Communion,
he does not allow them Communion at this time, but
waits until the end of the Liturgy.

"Let us rise!" On our feet physically, but on our spiritual feet in particular! That is to say, our minds should not be on lowly things, on small and sinful thoughts, but like golden eagles, all the faithful should be raised to the heights, making brilliant circles around Christ the Sun. The Mysteries are divine, holy, pure, immortal, heavenly and awesome. And because they are so, a deep and sincere "Thank You" should come from the Christian heart that has received Holy Communion.

This feeling of deep gratitude for Holy Communion is expressed in the following silent prayer of the priest:

"We thank Thee, O merciful Master and Lover of our souls, that Thou hast this day vouchsafed to give us Thy heavenly and immortal Mysteries; direct us into the right way, strengthen all of us in Thy fear, watch over our life, make our footsteps safe, through the prayers and supplications of the glorious Mother of God and ever-virgin Mary and of all Thy Saints."

"We thank Thee, O Lover of our souls." We thank You also for other benefits, known and unknown, but especially for enabling us to receive the Holy Mysteries today. This benefit is the highest of all. No other can be compared with this one. Christ in our hearts!

From now on our lives must be on a path where all our steps are Christian ones. Where Christ walks, we must follow. No deviations, no loss of direction from Christ's path. Is this an easy task? O Lord, we ask for Your help, "Direct us in the right way." Make our lives Christian ones. Strengthen us in Your fear. Hold us under the wings of Your divine love. You are our fortress, our strength, our protection. Make our path a safe one.

We ask for all this, O Lord, through the prayers of Your all-holy, ever-virgin Mother and all Your Saints, who are now safe in the untroubled harbor of Eternity and are praying for us who are in the turbulent sea of this life.

We thank You, Lover of our souls. Holy Communion is such a great benefit, that, as I once read, if there were only one church in the whole world that offered the Holy Eucharist, we should do our best to go there to receive the Body and Blood of our Lord. But now there is no need to travel far and spend money to receive Holy Communion. There are thousands of churches in Orthodoxy, and often our parish church is near – only a few steps away. And in spite of this, many never come to church to receive Communion and never thank the Lover of our souls.

As we said before, we should receive Communion worthily. For, as great a blessing as one receives in worthy participation in the Mystery, so great is the loss we suffer when we receive it unworthily. I once read that the unbelieving Saracens, wishing to mock the Holy Mysteries, took them and threw them to the dogs, but the dogs turned and attacked the Saracens, tearing them to pieces.

Let us pay attention, dear readers, how we receive Holy Communion and when God enables us to partake of them, let us thank Him from the bottoms of our hearts.

"DO THOU IN RETURN GLORIFY THEM"

As we saw in our last homily, after Holy Communion, the priest says the Prayer of Thanksgiving: "We thank Thee, O merciful Master. . . ." And at the end of this prayer, he says: "For Thou art our sanctification and to Thee we ascribe glory, to the Father and to the Son and to the Holy Spirit, now and forever and unto ages of ages." What does this exclamation mean?

What, dear friends is our purpose for living? According to the inspired teaching of Holy Scripture, the purpose of our lives is sanctification; that is, to throw away the old man, the evil in us, and put on the new man, virtue − to live a Christian life, one as Christ did, and to be awarded the Kingdom of Heaven. This purpose in life is not felt by many people, however.

Most people live for other purposes. Some live for riches; others, for pleasures and amusements; some for fame and glory; and still others for knowledge. There is no thought of sanctification or eternal life. Others, however, believe in Christ and listen to His divine teaching, for they know that beyond any worldly purpose, there is a divine purpose for living, i.e. to become holy. "Be ye holy; for I am holy" (Lev. 20:7, I Peter 1:16).

Sanctification is the greatest purpose for living. Without sanctification, everyting else is vain and perishable. Life only has meaning when it is intent on this purpose. To be sanctified, to become like a small

Christ on earth and be given the Kingdom of Heaven! The beast which lives inside us, the proud ego has to be annihilated, and we must become Christs to destroy the hells which our lives now are, and make them into heavens.

Sanctification is our highest purpose, but is it easy? Certainly not! If it were easy, Christ would not have come to earth. He came to open the way to heaven. He came to make us holy. Without Christ there would be no moral or religious improvement, and no salvation. Christ is all.

That which we offer for our sanctification is our will, our good intention: it is saying: "We want to be saved, I want to be sanctified." If our sanctification and salvation could be represented by the number 100, then 99.99% of this is Christ's work, the rest is our cooperation (0.01%). For this reason we address God and say: "Thou art our sanctification," and to Thee Father, Son, and Holy Spirit belongs all honor and glory, forever.

After this exclamation, the priest turns to the people and says, "Let us go forth in peace," which is to say, 'the Liturgy has ended, now it is time to leave the church, but with peaceful hearts; let us pray to God for this.' The priest then says the prayer called "The Prayer Behind the Ambon." It is called this because, in the ancient Church, when the Ambon was in the middle of the church, the priest stood behind it to say this prayer. But now, the Ambon being in another place, this prayer is said outside the Holy Sanctuary before the icon of our Lord. This prayer is as follows:

"O Lord, who blessest those who bless Thee and sanctifiest those who put their trust in Thee, save Thy people and bless Thine inheritance; protect the whole body of Thy Church and sanctify those who love the beauty of Thy House. Do Thou in return glorify them by Thy divine power and forsake not us who set our hope in Thee. Grant peace to Thy churches, to the priesthood, to our rulers, to the armed Forces and all Thy people. For all good giving and every perfect gift is from above, coming down from Thee, the Father of Lights; and to Thee we ascribe glory and thanksgiving and worship, to the Father and to the Son and to the Holy Spirit, now and ever and unto ages of ages."

In this beautiful prayer, the priest asks God to bless the people, all those who set their hope in God. He prays that God protect the whole body of the Church. But what is this "Whole Body?" The individuals who are on a sailing ship. There is the captain, the crew and the passengers. All these make the 'body.' The Church is also a type of ship which travels through the centuries. It has a body of clergy and laity; the clergy direct the ship in Christ's name, and the people are the passengers going to their eternal destination. Without clergy, there is no Church, but then again without people, the Church has no place to go. Both clergy and laity constitute the Church. The priest prays to God to protect and bless all those who love the beauty of His House, in other words, that those who take care of the church have all the materials necessary to perform the Sacraments and keep it clean and bright. We must confess that even in this impious age, there are poor people who give of their meager earnings to build and maintain churches.

Thus, people show their love of God both in words and deeds, and as they honor and glorify God, the priest entreats God to glorify them too, by His divine power. "Do Thou in return glorify them." And just as the planets face the sun and shine from the sun's light, so the faithful who turn towards Christ receive divine light. Christ's light reflects off of them and they become Christ's lights in the world and will shine like the sun in the world to come.

O Lord, bless, protect and glorify Your people!

Finally, the priest prays for peace in "the whole world," for the army and our civil authorities, that God guide them to do good.

For every good thing in the Church and the world, O Blessed Trinity, comes from You.

ANTIDORON: THE GIFT INSTEAD OF THE GIFTS

Immediately after the Prayer Behind the Ambon, the cantors chant "Blessed be the name of the Lord, from now and to the Ages." Whose words are these? During the Divine Liturgy, aside from the words of Christ and the Apostles, we heard words which were said by angels and archangels, some by kings and simple people, others by prophets and saints. The words we hear now were first said by a great Old Testament figure, Job the victorious.

We all know his story. He was struck by great misfortunes. His house was destroyed, all his property perished. His children, seven boys and three girls met horrible death inside the house. In spite of all this, however, Job remained steadfast in his faith. He uttered no bitter words against God; He did not blaspheme. But what did he say? "Blessed be the name of the Lord" (Job 1:21).

The example Job gives us is that, no matter what our situation might be, and no matter how many sorrows and temptations we encounter, we should always, from the bottoms of our hearts, give words of thanks to God. God is all-good, and can make bitter things sweet. Everything that happens to us, be it bitter or sweet, has its purpose for our salvation. "Blessed," therefore, "be the name of the Lord, from this time forth and forevermore."

While this is chanted, the priest goes to the Prothesis and says:

"O Christ our God, who art Thyself the fulfillment of the Law and the Prophets, and hast fulfilled all the dispensation of the Father, do Thou always fill our hearts with joy and gladness, now and forever and from all Ages to all Ages. Amen."

This is to say, O Christ, all the prophecies of the Old Testament are fulfilled in You. The Hebrews who do not believe in You still wait, in vain, for the Messiah about whom their prophecies speak. The Messiah has come. You are He. The prophecies can apply to none other than You, and all that the Law had commanded concerning sacrifice and holocausts were mere shadows of Your person and redemptive work. Everything begins in You and ends in You. You are the Alpha and the Omega, the Beginning and the End; You are the fullness and fulfillment. Whatever had to be done for the world's salvation has been done by You – You accomplished the Father's Mystery of Divine Economy.

Christ, what wondrous things we saw and heard! Fill our hearts with joy and gladness, a prelude to what we will experience in that blessed life to come, when we will drink anew from the Cup of Life.

After this silent prayer, the priest invites the people to prayer for the last time: "Let us pray to the Lord," and says:

"May the blessing of the Lord and His mercy come upon you through His Divine grace and love for mankind; always, now and forever and unto ages of ages."

Then he says the Dismissal:

"Glory to Thee, O God, our hope, glory to Thee. May Christ, our true God, Who rose from the dead, have mercy upon us, through the intercession of His most pure and holy Mother; through the power of the precious and life-giving Cross; the protection of the sublime spiritual powers of heaven; the supplications of the holy glorious Prophet and Forerunner John the Baptist; of the holy, glorious and most honored Apostles; of the holy, glorious and victorious Martyrs; of our saintly and God-inspired Fathers; of the holy and righteous ancestors of God, Joachim and Anna; the Saint whose memory we celebrate today, and all the Saints; and may Christ save us, for He is gracious and loveth mankind.

"Through the prayers of our holy Fathers, have mercy upon us, O Lord Jesus Christ our God. Amen."

Thus ends the Divine Liturgy. The priest distributes Antidoron before the Beautiful Gate. What is Antidoron? As we said before, in ancient times all the faithful used to receive Holy Communion. There was no Antidoron as there is today. Antidoron (instead of the Gifts) is given now to Christians who do not receive the Holy Mysteries. It is given to them instead of the Gift. The Gift that is greater than all the world's treasures is Holy Communion, the holy Body and precious Blood of Christ. Nothing else can replace this Mystery. Compared to this Gift, Antidoron is a piece of glass next to a diamond. I pray that those holy times will return, when only those who have a penance will refrain from receiving Holy Communion! Certainly, the Antidoron gives some blessing, but the true blessing is in the Mystery of Mysteries, Holy Communion.

We have observed yet another source of disorder in the church. As soon as people hear: "Through the prayers...," they begin greeting each other and talking, which destroys the atmosphere of the Divine Liturgy.

Unfortunately, we have no awakened conscience. If we did, we would be aware of the miracle that took place in the Liturgy, and everyone would be under the influence of this experience; for when the soul is astonished by great things, it usually remains in silent admiration. Therefore, Christians should leave the church silently and in admiration, to spread over the land like apostles and say: "O world, see what you are losing by not receiving Holy Communion! Why do you live in darkness? Come to church."

"Come, O faithful, and receive from the unwaning light!"

Yes, true Christians desire to worship God "in spirit and truth" (John 4:24) during the Divine Liturgy! With Christians who are conscientious and reborn, the world would once again see the *Miracle*, and would believe in and return to Christ.

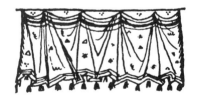

INDEX

✛   ✚   ✛

CRCRCRCRCRCRCRCRCRCRCRCRCR

OTHER BOOKS AUTHORED BY
AUGOUSTINOS N. KANTIOTES,
BISHOP OF FLORINA

1. *St. Cosmas Aitolos (Kosmas ho Aitolos)*, 7th ed., 426 pp., Athens, 1986.
2. *From the Unwaning Light (Ek tou Anesperous Photos)*, 248 pp., Volos, 1950.
3. *Toward Golgotha (Pros ton Golgotha)*, 3rd ed., 304 pp., Athens, 1975.
4. *Trumpet Calls (Salpismata)*, 208 pp., Athens, 1952. (Out of print.)
5. *Signs of the Times (Semeia ton Kairon)*, 240 pp. Athens, 1953. (Out of print.)
6. *A Free and Vibrant Church (Eleuthera kai Zosa Ekklesia)*, 212 pp., Athens, 1955. (Out of print.)
7. *For Country Folk (Pros ten Hypaithron)*, 64 pp., Athens, 1955. (Out of print.)
8. *The Four Colors (Ta Tessera Chromata)*, 224 pp., Athens, 1956. (Out of print.)
9. *Image and Reality (Eikones kai Pragmatikotetes)*, Part I, 192 pp., Athens, 1957. (Out of print.)
10. *The Pearl of Great Price (Ho Polytimos Margarites)*, 352 pp., Athens, 1958. (Out of print.)
11. *St. Synkletike (Hagia Synkletike)*, 100 pp., Athens, 1959. (Out of print).
12. *An Abominable Slander (Mia Bdelyra Sykophantia)*, 80 pp., Athens, 1960.
13. *National Problems (Ethnika Problemata)*, 336 pp., Athens, 1961.

14. *Image and Reality (Eikones kai Pragmatikotites)*, Part II, 320 pp., Athens, 1962. (Out of print.)

15. *The Contemporary Religious and Moral Situation (He Synchronos Threkseutike kai Ethike Katastasis)*, 112 pp., Athens, 1964. (Out of print.)

16. *The Preacher's Apology (Apologia tou Hierokerykos)*, 368 pp., Athens, 1965.

17. *Follow Me (Akolouthei Moi)*, 2nd ed., 504 pp., Athens, 1970. (Out of print.)

18. *Time and the Four Seasons (Ho Chronos kai hai Tessares Epochai)*, 164 pp., Athens, 1966. (Out of print).

19. *Greece's Educational Problem (To Ekpaideutikon Problema tes Hellados)*, 208 pp., Athens, 1967. (Out of print).

20. *Miracles (Ta Thaumata)*, 304 pp., Athens, 1968. (Out of print.)

21. *Ecclesiastical Memoranda (Ekklesiastika Hypomnemata)*, 208 pp., Athens, 1969.

22. *To the Clergy and Laity (Pros Kleron kai Laon)*, 432 pp., Athens, 1969.

23. *National Anniversaries (Ethnikai Epeteioi)*, 320 pp., Athens, 1970.

24. *Battle Against Blasphemy (Agon Kata tes Blasphemias)*, 192 pp., Athens, 1971.

25. *An Account of a Four-Year Perid (Apologismos mias Tetraetias)*, 304 pp., Athens, 1971. (Out of print.)

26. *The Lord's Day (Kyriake)*, 276 pp., Athens, 1972.

27. *The Church's Ostrich Policy (Ekklesiastikos Strouthdkamelismos)*, 224 pp., Athens, 1972.

28. *To the Christian Flock (Pros to Christeponymon Pleroma)*, 544 pp., Athens, 1973.

29. *Answers to Church Concerns (Apanteseis epi Ekklesiastikon Thematon)*, 96 pp., Athens, 1973.

30. *Book of Apostolic Excerpts (Apostolos)*, 286 pp., Athens, 1973.

31. *Chronicle of a Current Crisis (Chronikon Sobouses Kriseos)*, 128 pp., Athens, 1973.

32. *We Were Astonished (Exestemen)*, 141 pp., Athens, 1973.

33. *Sweet Smelling Flowers (Myripnoa Anthe)*, 278 pp., Athens, 1974.
34. *Social Sores (Koinonikai Plegai)*, 2nd ed., 288 pp., Athens, 1986.
35. *To My Flock (Pros to Poimnion)*, 459 pp., Athens, 1975.
36. *An Account of the Second Four-Year period (Apologismos Deuteras Tetraetias)*, 350 pp., Athens, 1976.
37. *The Orthodox House of Worship (Orthodoxos Naos)*, 260 pp., Athens, 1976.
38. *On the Divine Liturgy (Eis ten Theian Leitourgian)*, Part I, 346 pp., Athens, 1977.
39. *The Thorn Reigns (Basileuei to Ankathi)*, 441 pp., Athens, 1978.
40. *On the Divine Liturgy (Eis ten Theian Leitourgian)*, Part II, 352 pp., Athens, 1978.
41. *The Sea (He Thalassa)*, 384 pp., Athens, 1979.
42. *From All Walks of Life (Ap' Hola ta Epangelmata)*, 288 pp., Athens, 1980.
43. *Divorce (To Diazygion)*, 192 pp., Athens, 1980.
44. *An Account of the Third Four-Year Period (Apologismos Trites Tetraetias)*, 560 pp., Athens, 1980.
45. *Reminders (Hypomneseis)*, 438 pp., Athens, 1980.
46. *"Turn the TV Off!" ('Kleiste tis Teleoraseis!')*, 158 pp., Athens, 1981.
47. *Our Macedonia (He Makedonia mas)*, 208 pp., Athens, 1982.
48. *Drops from the Living Water (Stagones Apo to Hydor to Zon)*, 2nd ed., 316 pp., Athens, 1986.
49. *Sparks from the Book of Apostolic Excerpts (Spintheres apo ton Apostolo)*, 320 pp., Athens, 1983.
50. *A Cross-Examination (Ho Elenchos)*, 218 pp., Athens, 1983.
51. *An Account of the Fourth Four-Year Period (Apologismos Tetartes Tetraetias)*, 606 pp., Athens, 1984.
52. *Shepherd's Pipe (Phlogera)*, 300 pp., Athens, 1985.
53. *Free? (Eleutheroi?)*, 174 pp., Athens, 1986.
54. *Miscellany (Poikila)*, 416 pp., Athens, 1986.

SOME OTHER BOOKS PUBLISHED BY
THE INSTITUTE FOR BYZANTINE
AND MODERN GREEK STUDIES

*MODERN ORTHODOX SAINTS, Vol. 9,
ST. METHODIA OF KIMOLOS*

Remarkable Ascetic, Teacher of Virtue, Counselor, Comforter
and Healer (1865-1908). An account of her Life, Character,
Miracles and Influence, together with Selected Hymns from
the Akolouthia in honor of her, and a Letter to her sister
Anna. By Constantine Cavarnos. Publication date: November
1986. Illus.
ISBN-0-914744-75-5 (Clothbound), 0-914744-76-3 (Paperbound).

AN EXPLORER OF REALMS OF ART, LIFE, AND THOUGHT

A survey of the works of philosopher and theologian Constantine Cavarnos. In this book, Dr. John E. Rexine, Charles A.
Dana Professor of the Classics and Chairman of the Depart-
ment of the Classics at Colgate University, focuses on 33 books
by Dr. Cavarnos published between 1949 and 1985, discussing them in as many chapters in a clear, concise, and engag-
ing manner. In addition, he gives valuable information about
Cavarnos' life and concerns as an educator and writer, and
a Bibliography listing all of the latter's books and pamphlets,
selected articles, reviews and translations. 1985, 184 pp.,
many illus.
ISBN 0-914744-69-0 (Clothbound), 0-914744-70-4 (Paperbound).

Clothbound $9.00
Paperbound $6.00

A DIALOGUE BETWEEN BERGSON, ARISTOTLE, AND PHILOLOGOS

"Originally printed in 1949, this work was the winner of a prestigious Bowdoin Prize at Harvard University in 1947, and constitutes Constantine Cavarnos' 'first book.'" In this dialogue, the basic and dominant questions are: "What is that ever-present dynamism and change with which the whole world of nature is always pulsating? What is that rational insight or awareness which is the peculiar possession of man?" There is a preface by Professor John Wild of Harvard, introductory remarks by C.D. Georgoulis, leading Athenian philosopher, and comments by C.I. Lewis and Raphael Demos, Professors of Philosophy at Harvard. Third, enlarged edition. Publication date: October 1986.
ISBN 0-914744-77-1 (Paperbound).

PLATO'S VIEW OF MAN

Two Bowen Prize essays dealing with the problem of the destiny of man and the individual life in Plato's philosophy, together with selected passages from his dialogues on man and the human soul, newly translated from the ancient Greek. By Dr. C. Cavarnos. 2nd printing, 1982. 95 pp.
ISBN 0-914744-26-7   Paperbound $3.50

PLATO'S THEORY OF FINE ART

Plato's general theory of fine art and a critical examination of specific fine arts: architecture, sculpture, painting, the dance, music, rhetoric, narrative, comedy, tragedy, lyric and epic poetry. Also, an anthology of passages on the fine arts and the beautiful, compiled from Plato's dialogues and translated from the ancient Greek texts. By C. Cavarnos. 1973. 98 pp.
ISBN 0-914744-45-3 (Clothbound), 0-914744-46-1 (Paperbound)

Clothbound $6.00
Paperbound $3.50

MODERN GREEK THOUGHT

Three essays by C. Cavarnos dealing with Greek thought from 1750 to the present. The first is an introduction to modern Greek philosophy through a discussion of its distinctive characteristics. The other essays discuss the standpoint of many outstanding intellectuals − philosophers, theologians, scientists, poets, novelists and others − regarding the capabilities and value of the positive sciences and the questions of the nature and destiny of man. 1969. 115 pp.
ISBN 0-914744-10-0   Paperbound $4.50

PAMPHLETS

BYZANTINE SACRED MUSIC

A concise treatment of the essential characteristics, aims, and execution of the traditional, official music of the Greek Orthodox Church. By Prof. C. Cavarnos. 4th printing, 1981. 31 pp.
ISBN 0-914744-23-2 $1.25

ST. GREGORY OF NYSSA ON THE ORIGIN AND DESTINY OF THE SOUL

This is a portion of Prof. John P. Cavarnos' Harvard doctoral dissertation, entitled *The Psychology of Gregory of Nyssa*. 3rd printing, 1982. 12 pp.
ISBN 0-914744-60-7 $1.00

THE ICON

Texts on the spiritual basis and purpose of holy icons by St. John Damascene and the Seventh Oecumenical Synod, translated by Prof. Constantine Cavarnos, together with an Introduction by him. 6th printing, 1986. 11 pp., 2 illus.
ISBN 0-914744-19-4 $1.00